Thor

Incense
and
Incense Rituals

Healing Ceremonies for Spaces of Subtle Energy
Handbook with Best Methods and Substances

Translated by Christine M. Grimm

LOTUS PRESS
SHANGRI-LA

Disclaimer
The information presented in this book has been carefully researched and passed on to our best knowledge and conscience. Despite this fact neither the author nor the publisher assume any type of liability for presumed or actual damage to any person that might result from the direct application or use of the statements in this book. The information in this book is solely intended for interested readers and educational purposes.

List of Sources:
Photos of the incense substances: Thomas Kinkele
"Burning incense," ©by Primavera Life, photographed by Ulla Mayer-Raichle, page 7 & 21
"Dancing Group," illustration by Stefan Salis, page 39
"Unity of the Three," illustration by Soham Holger Gerull, page 43
"Amida Buddha," illustration by Petra Könner, page 47
"Healing Spirits," ©by Jabrane M. Sebnat, painted by Elisabeth Brandi, page 59

First English Edition 2004
© Lotus Press
Box 325, Twin Lakes, WI 53181, USA
website: www.lotuspress.com
email: lotuspress@lotuspress.com
The Shangri-La Series is published in cooperation
with Schneelöwe Verlagsberatung, Federal Republic of Germany
© 2001 by Windpferd Verlagsgesellschaft mbH, Aitrang, Germany
All rights reserved
Translated by Christine M. Grimm
Edited by Neehar Douglass
Cover design by Kuhn Graphik, Digitales Design, Zürich, Switzerland,
by using a photo by: Ulla Mayer-Raichle, ©Primavera Life

ISBN 0-914955-76-4
Printed in Germany

Table of Contents

Introduction to Incense Burning

A great revival is happening. A tradition that has played an esoteric part in many of the enduring cultures of our planet is now spreading like wildfire.

The practice of burning aromatic plants can be traced back through every culture of humankind on earth. Its purpose has always been in some way related to the preservation of life. It may be to promote physical, mental or emotional well being or for protection against infection. It may be a meaningful method of preserving foods or as a companion for religious, spiritual or even magical ceremonies.

Anyone who catches a whiff of aromatic smoke is stirred deeply. Reactions to it are obviously quite diverse, the sensations frequently connecting with elemental experiences. From archaic instincts to pleasant or even unpleasant childhood experiences, many different aspects of our inner life may become activated indicating a clear response to the presence of an aromatic fragrance.

For someone whose childhood has been spent around a smokehouse the fragrance of beech and juniper smoke could be intensely interwoven with personal inner images. Regardless of whether the associations it provides are pleasant or unpleasant a statement about the emotional quality of this childhood has been evoked. It may be expressed in a number of different ways but the message will always be completely authentic.

The smoke of aromatic plants appears to have some sort of key effect on us. Something is locked in the basement and longs to be set free. The impression that a fragrance brings seems to manifest within us something that demands a place of its own.

Really, its amazing that so many of us are suddenly into burning incense, as though a quality somehow lost on the path through the recent past is seeking to be remembered, to be recovered and included once again in our lives.

Wherever the warm/spicy, sweet/aromatic or tangy/woody fragrances of incense unfold time seems to stand still. We stop our mechanical mundane activities and for a short moment dwell in the timeless presence of sensory perception. This impression is often so intense as to be surprising. Continuing on our way we sometimes sense that a small transformation has occurred—an experience to make us more aware of ourselves.

Experimenting with incense burning will open up a whole world of interesting and helpful impressions. You can do it on your own, using this book to inspire you, or you can plunge more deeply into the phenomenon with a guide who offers work in this medium to the public.

Where Did Incense Burning Originate?

Plant derived aromas are used in a great variety of ways, giving rise to many customs. A day without fragrance, so the saying went in Ancient Egypt, was a day lost. Olibanum was burned in the morning, myrrh at noon and a carefully prepared incense called *kyphi* in the evening.

Kyphi was said to be the incense for relaxation and the mild evenings of an ancient Egyptian city were filled with sweet, aromatic and sensual billowings from thousands of homes, combining into a symphony of fragrances with great variety of nuance.

Kyphi, as reported by the Roman historian Plutarch (A.D. 100.) was burned at night. Gently it would rock people to sleep, evoke dreams and drive away the worries of the day. It conveyed peace and tranquility to those inhaling it—a wonderful idea. Even today you can share in these sensations if you can manage to catch the scent of a good *kyphi* cocktail which, according to fragments of the traditional recipe, consisted of more than twelve aromatic ingredients. The sweet, spicy, aromatic clouds of this fragrant smoke do great justice to the expression 'nectar of the gods'.

Sensitivity to detail plays such a special role in both the spiritual and secular life of the Japanese that it's natural to expect them to have developed an incense burning culture of sophisticated esthetics. Respect for life and the joy of BEING find their expression in a tradition where the most precious aromatic plants such as eaglewood *(Jinkoh)* and sandalwood are burned in tiny portions with precision-made utensils. Sensory delight stimulating the imagination leads to the high art of *Koh-do*. In *Koh-do* there is a fragrance ceremony in which selected individuals seek to intensify both their awareness and inspiration.

Incense burning traditions amongst the Native Americans see a cosmic presence in 'power plants' like white and gray sage, juniper and cedar, helping restore people's contact with nature as a whole and with the Great Spirit.

So impressive is this panorama that the rediscovery of such a fascinating medium and its reintroduction to our civilized Western culture becomes imperative.

However its revival also contains a darker side. There are for example people who will intensely reject everything found under the collective term 'frankincense'. These gut reactions are sometimes quite vehement and can include both spontaneous nausea and aggression. In such cases the Church has most often played a role.

The heavy use of frankincense in Catholic liturgical rituals (usually recipes of olibanum, myrrh, tolu balsam, benzoin, mastic, labdanum and dragon blood) has often done a very thorough job during the childhood of someone affected in this way. Intense fragrance related impressions can have extreme effect on the childhood psyche. The threat of a God who punishes sin, compulsion and the violation of His laws has subliminally linked the fragrance of the burning incense with emotional fear and constriction. This may trigger intensely defensive gut reactions later in life.

The same applies to many emotionally reactive patterns that a fragrance may evoke. What these reactions reveal is the conditioning imprinted via such early experiences. The fragrance comes to represent the threat or stress. It reflects content that corresponds to unpleasant, pain-related experiences. The good news is that we can dissolve these patterns.

It is interesting to note how what we perceive is usually judged in absolute terms. A person will say 'this does not smell good', believing that he or she has made an objective statement. This becomes more obvious when the enthusiastic response of the next person to the same fragrance shows up the first opinion for what it really is, purely subjective.

Incidentally this endless polarizing of good versus bad is also the territory out of which the exoteric religions have developed, dictating guidelines as to what should be called good or evil. In this context pleasant scents correspond to the divine while a foul smell is considered to be the work of the devil. How purely subjective such absolute statements are becomes self evident when, as in the case of frankincense, the judgment is turned into its opposite by the next person.

Quite probably we all carry a primeval motivating experience in our <u>instinctive</u> center. In terms of human development this experience extends back to the Stone Age. The German author Christian Rätsch describes it very interestingly as a personal ritual experience in *Räucherstoffe—Der Atem des Drachen:*

"Our ancestors sought out caves for their rites where, gathered around a fire and invoking their deities they told mythological stories. Twigs of aromatic plants burning in the flames gave off fragrances that carried these people into transcendental spaces. These experiences of oneness led them to deep connection with existence. It is probable that this is the origin of genuine feelings of sacredness."

States that extend beyond physical existence in time and space leave deep impressions on the human psyche. Such experiences meld with fragrance, thus creating traditions which mythologically assigned particular deities to certain plants. Even today fire and smoke are still deeply rooted in the primeval human instinct. And at this point we gain access to a great truth.

Fire

Fire is an elemental force uniting the beginning and the end within itself. It is the force of change. In the world of nature it destroys what is old and creates fertile ground for rebirth. Human encounter with fire is also confrontation with human fear. Overcoming fear is a major issue in the face of this regenerative power. For primeval humans mastering this force gave them both warmth and protection from wild animals.

During the past 20 years shamanic healing rituals such as <u>firewalking</u> and <u>sweat lodge ceremonies</u> have found a certain acceptance in our modern cultures. They seem to awaken a sense of the archaic, evoking a new sense of awareness. To perceive the purification that occurs in the presence of fire and to find a sense of peace deep within is to experience a <u>rebirth.</u> Courage and capacity are ignited within when a human being encounters his *very own* fire.

The great traditional fire ceremonies in Europe take place during the solstice. The vast cycles of light show us the rhythms of nature to which all living beings on our earth are subject.

Whenever we are responsible for a fire we are also obliged to be attentive and cautious. Continually it reminds us of the transience of life on earth, seeking to make us aware of our adventure through the arena of perception where we are so wonderfully integrated into life's cycle. A process in which free will and responsibility are inseparably bound.

The teachings of fire are very direct. Its notorious unpredictability has triggered many a catastrophe. Yet always it represents the truth of the transience of physical life and is a reminder of the moment of transformation.

The foremost principle in establishing a true friendship with the element of fire is to treat it with respect. This friendship is so full of blessings however that it is worth every effort to pay it the necessary respect.

RESPECT

The Fire Source for Burning Incense

Whenever we burn plant material we need of course to use fire. A flame or embers are necessary to transform the plant body into fragrant smoke. Whether we apply fire as glowing coals or as a candle flame will depend upon our purpose in burning the incense. You will discover much more about this in the section on 'Methods and Utensils'.

If you get a chance to sit before an open fire today don't you feel the magic, the fascination which radiates from this powerful element? Spellbound by the consuming dynamics of a fire as it crackles and spits we watch it devouring every morsel that the greedy flames can reach. Even in the figurative sense this element serves by ridding us of the old and used. It makes possible new beginnings.

At this point I would like to give a more detailed description of the alchemical aspects which play an important part in the burning of incense.

In keeping with everything that we learn about the origin of incense burning, fragrance is a subtle force which can influence all centers of perception (gut/instinct/body, heart/emotion/soul and mind/thought/spirit). Fire is that energy through which the process of refinement is triggered. The fragrance that emerges with the fading embers is as the soul of the plant released through this process.

Water rises up out of the earthly substance as a visible wisp of 'smoke' and carries with it this plant-soul as a fragrance impression. It is an alchemical process of transformation. A refinement is taking place in which the essence of the plant is separated from its gross material body and through a process of chemistry becomes accessible to our sensory perception as an ethereal substance.

One's sense of smell affects both the psychological and emotional realms. This can prove to be a true blessing. However a respectful approach to the process is the prerequisite for a pleasant and meaningful experience.

The Effect of Burning Incense

When fragrance molecules attach to the sensitive endings of the olfactory nerves (the only direct contact that our neurons have with the outside world) they are immediately transmitted by the olfactory bulb as electric nerve impulses to the limbic system. The result is an emotional reaction that we may perceive as liking or disliking.

There are also times when we are not capable of making a clear judgment. Our feelings vacillate only to discover a slowly developing appeal in the impression of a fragrance that we had at first tended to reject. This is a reaction similar to those in many other aspects of life.

The limbic system is the headquarters of our emotional world. This is where all the information accumulated through the emotional conditioning of a lifetime is stored. Light and darkness appear to reign between pleasure desire and pain, joy and fear, anger and fear, doubt and trust causing us to respond with acceptance or repulsion.

Reflex-like structures have developed, responding more quickly than the mental custodians in the cerebrum. This gives an emotional reaction a certain advantage over the more slowly generated ideas we create about ourselves and the world around us. This advantage is conferred thanks to the authenticity of the olfactory resonance.

"Our preference for a certain fragrance should be perceived as an expression of the body signaling a need for the qualities inherent therein.[2] The instinctive center reacts with the greatest speed. The very first perceptible impulse comes from this source.

Whenever we receive a clearly positive resonance from the instinctive center we can place our trust in that fragrance. It will support us and provide assistance in regulating imbalanced states. In effect we are open to the helpful inclination of this plant soul.

To the same degree a reaction of not liking or rejecting a fragrance implies the opposite. So we can see that the individual reaction to an incense fragrance must be the expression of an inner disposition, a willingness or not to open up to the characteristics of this fragrance. What makes the difference is a profound connection with the essence of the aromatic plant to which we are or are not open.

Being open to it, that is, being able to admit the impression shows a willingness to accept the regulatory impulses of the plant. We open ourselves to the power of the plant, welcome it and allow it to have its beneficial effect on our being.

Choose only those smells that cause your heart to sing. This way you can't go wrong. Once you begin to discover the path of fragrance you also find yourself attracted to those aromas which represent a certain mystery to you because you somehow appear to be denied access to them. You must find the key to them. It connects in directly with the search for self.

Everything that serves to dissolve tensions is supportive of life and brings us

closer to love. It is interesting to note that regularly using a pleasing incense creates exactly that effect because its regulating impulse harmonizes and stabilizes body, mind and soul. This effect of incense burning may be quite clearly perceived. We become more and more capable of opening up. Energy begins to flow freely and strength is created.

This usually means a greater acceptance of an incense that initially seemed unpleasant. A growing harmony develops within.

The exact nature of our experience when we expose ourselves to the fragrances of incense therefore varies considerably. On the one hand it depends on our state of mind, on the other however, it also depends on our intention in burning incense in the first place.

Whatever it is that I would like to discover, whatever problem I want to solve or even whichever occasion I would like to celebrate exerts a strong influence on the effectiveness of the incense burning.

Burning incense always creates a connection to the subtle levels, consequently carrying whatever concerns us into higher dimensions from where support and fulfillment seem to come. Prayers and good wishes are transported into otherworldly realms where they allow the true intention of the person burning the incense to unfold. In doing so we enter the metaphysical realm of the creative force from where all manifestations originate.[1]

Methods and Utensils for Burning Incense

To be able to integrate incense burning as a pleasant and easy part of everyday life, some meaningful and practical aids are needed.

Over thousands of years varieties of methods and procedures for preparing and burning of aromatic plants or material have been developed and preserved. However, traditional methods of burning incense tend to be similar all over the world. Methods and paraphernalia vary only with the esthetic sense of different cultures. Hence today throughout the world we find certain standard ways in which to burn incense.

Ways of Incense Burning

Incense Sticks

Incense sticks are common everywhere and are currently much in demand. They are such a practical way to create fragrant smoke. Light the stick at one end and blow the flame out after a few seconds if it doesn't go out by itself. The stick will now slowly burn down and release the aromatic scent in a fine wisp of smoke.

It is generally accepted that Buddhist monks in India developed this method of burning incense. There are typically two types of incense stick:

1. *With supporting wood:* This is a thin bamboo stick which is two-thirds covered with a moist paste ideally made of high quality aromatic woods such as red sandalwood and cedar. The wood

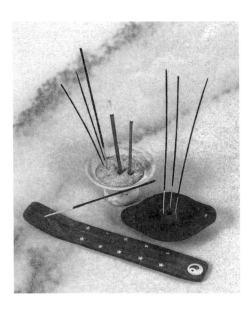

powder is mixed with tragacanth gum or liquid gum arabic as a binder.

Aromatic substances are then added, sometimes as solids but also frequently as essential oils. The incense sticks are ready when the paste has dried.

Nowadays it is common practice amongst Arabian, eastern Indian and Chinese producers to include fanciful perfumes to give their incense an exotic touch. They treat these recipes with great secrecy. In the process they generally don't make any distinction between synthetic and natural perfumes hence there is a lot of incense with an intense synthetic perfume on the market especially from India (*agarbatti*) and China (joss sticks).

When it comes to quality we simply have to trust our own noses since it's impossible to get hold of any authentic list of ingredients without a chemicophysical analysis.

In India top quality sticks are very thin ones with a fine coating. A whole variety of holders are available in order to burn them effectively.

During Buddhist celebrations and ceremonies, primarily in Far Eastern countries (Hong Kong, Thailand, Malaysia) very large incense sticks up to 2 meters (6 feet) in length are burned outdoors.

2. *Without wooden support:* The method in this case somewhat resembles the production of noodles. The prepared aromatic paste is squeezed out like a snake which becomes firm when it is dry. The advantage of these sticks is that there are no disturbing nuances of burning bamboo.

Especially pure and wholly natural outdoor incense sticks of this type come from the Tibetan tradition. Authentic **Healing Incense** sticks are today made in Nepal according to the original recipe using 31 plant substances as a traditional Tibetan medicine. They are known by the name *Agar 31* and have been handed down through the centuries in the Buddhist medicinal *Tantra* scriptures.

These incense sticks are made in a somewhat coarser way (Ø up to 2 inches), yet are considered to be most healing and free of side effects. Their fragrance is powerfully woody/spicy and they don't produce much smoke. It is really worth trying to get hold of the authentic potency because there is a lot of inferior quality also on offer. However if the quality is ensured by the supervision of a Tibetan physician the packages will contain a statement to this effect.

Agar 31 is reputed to be effective in treating fear of heights, headaches and nausea due to oxygen deficiency which, at altitudes of over 2000m where this tradition originated, is not unusual. Furthermore, it is said to be equally helpful in cases of mental exhaustion, stress, sleeplessness, back and chest pains, dry lips, muscular stiffness as well as pains of psychosomatic origin.

The relaxing and meditation promoting effects of this incense are highly valued by enthusiasts. Not only may the incense be burned, but for the

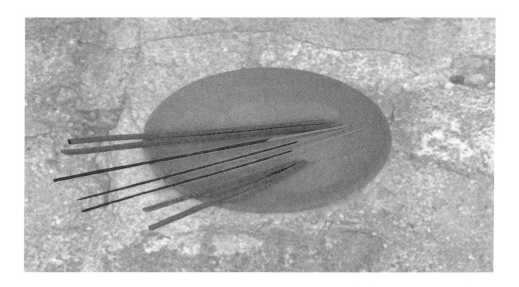

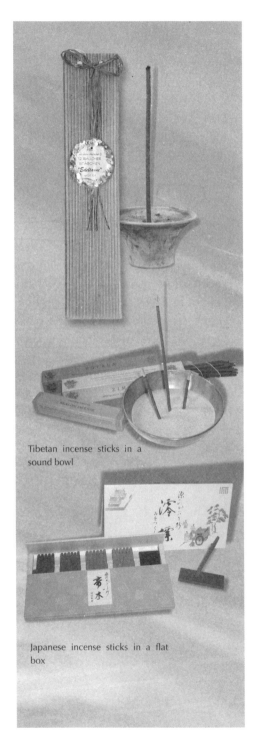

Tibetan incense sticks in a sound bowl

Japanese incense sticks in a flat box

relief of neuralgic complaints it may be finely ground and mixed together with a little vegetable oil for massage. This has an extremely warming and soothing effect.

Handmade Tibetan incense sticks are also available under the name of **Zimpo** (*Zhempus*) or **Potala.** They consist of 25 aromatic plant substances from the Himalayas. Red and white sandalwood, rhododendron, saffron, mugwort, galangal, nard root, cedar wood and costus root are among the traditionally used plants. These sticks are burned with the intention of encouraging an open state of mind, cleansing the air, protecting against negative influences and creating a loving and life affirming atmosphere.

A bowl filled with sand is especially well suited to burning these sticks. When enough fragrance has unfolded the sticks can be put out by simply turning them upside down in the sand, to be lit again at another time.

Ancient Japanese tradition offers a superior quality of incense without any supporting stick which is enjoying increasing popularity in the Western world. They are very delicate sticks, indicating a rather subtle and sophisticated form of incense culture. At the time when Buddhism was introduced in the 6th Century Japan also took up the use of exquisite incense from China. These aromatic fragrances soon found their way from religious contexts into the world of sensory pleasures as well as the arts.

Training the mind to perceive beauty has always been the ethical foundation of high Japanese culture. _Listening to the fragrance is_ an active form of attaining inspiration and sensitivity. _Koh-do,_ the _path of burning incense_ developed from this background and accordingly produced particularly esthetic varieties of incense.

Small holders to support these exquisite sticks of incense as they burn are usually included in the package. The price range of these products usually lies at the top end of the market especially when they are made of finely ground precious wood such as eaglewood (jinkoh) and white sandalwood.

After mixing these with other select ground aromatic substances such as cloves, anise, cinnamon, sunset hibiscus seeds (hibiscus abelmusk) and frankincense, adding hot water plus the gummy bark of the tabuko tree a dough is made out of which the sticks are then pressed.

Exclusive manufacturers do not use synthetic fragrances or binders in the production process, cheaper incense however may contain them. In Japan the exact composition of these creations has always been a well kept secret.

Incense Spirals

The incense spiral is another product that is made in the same way as these unsupported sticks. This type of incense has the advantage of burning for a very long time, which makes it popular especially where large spaces like temple halls are to be imbued with fragrance.

Very large spirals with diameters of up to 16 inches and a burning time of 24 hours are produced in India specifically to repel insects. Sweet grass citronella (cymbopogon nardus) is usually included as the aromatic substance. These large spirals come with fine strings attached and can be hung so ingeniously that only the ash falls off and the halter stays in place to the very end. There are special stands for burning small spirals.

Incense spirals and holder

17

Incense Cones and Other Shapes

One of the most widespread and common types of incense is the cone. Simply lit at the tip, it then smolders on its own for about 20 minutes. Incense cones are made in Europe as well as in India, Indonesia, China and Japan. The Giant Mountains of Saxony in Germany produce what are known as 'Incense Figurines' and ceramic artifacts designed to hold the cones as they spread their fragrance, particularly at Christmastime. With growing interest in aromatic modes this old regional tradition is spreading to other European countries.

The cones are very simple to burn. Since they do not develop much heat they can easily be ignited on a small ceramic plate, a practical way for travelers who wish to enjoy a familiar fragrance during a stopover.

An even more sophisticated approach is to cut and form exquisite shapes from the rolled paste using special tools. It is no surprise that such delicately esthetic details are particularly valued in the Japanese culture.

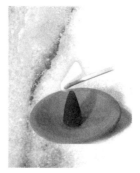

Lighting an incense cone

Native American Smudges

In the Native American tradition plants known as _power herbs_ are burned as smudges. This involves cutting certain twigs, bushes and herbs 'in the right way' and then drying them. They are tied into bundles about 8-12 inches long and hung up for a considerable period of time in a dark airy place so that they dry completely. Cutting herbs in _the right way_ means approaching them with mindfulness and respect for the well being and life of the plants. This involves not causing any unnecessary stress and thanking them for the gift of their vital energy.

The dried and tightly bound smudges are lit at the tip until they are really burning and then waved through the air so that the flame dies and they glow vigorously as their pungent herbal fragrance unfolds. Teepees, sacred sites, objects of daily use and of course the body become enveloped in the aromatic smoke and cleansed of all negative influences.

Cedar tips (Western cedar tips)

Juniper twig tips (Juniperus tips)

Gray sage (desert Sage)

White sage

These are the classic power herbs which are burned as described above.

Sweet grass is braided and then lit at the end.

One of the special Native American incense accessories is the abalone shell. Usually 4 to 8 inches across, with its mother-of-pearl luster it beautifully serves to hold the burning herbs or smoldering bundles. The natural holes which are strung like pearls under the shell's edge allow a sufficient supply of air for the glowing embers.

Mellie Uyldert thinks that the preferred approach is to create and dry mixed smudging bundles from native aromatic plants like juniper twig tips, sage, lavender, cedar tips, thyme, savory, lemon balm, rosemary etc. Often just what is best for us in a certain moment falls into our hands. Shamanic holistic medicine assumes that exactly the right herb needed to help restore the organism to balance will be growing in that person's own garden.*

Allowing the aromatic smoke of home-made smudges to take effect may guide one back to one's own full power.

Incense paste in leaf form.

ABALONE

Ways of Incense Burning

* Mellie Uyldert, *The Physic Garden—Plants and Their Esoteric Relationship with Man,* Thorsen.

Smudges and sweet-grass braid

Burning Pure Aromatic
Plant Substances

The fourth chapter of this book introduces a great variety of aromatic plants that are used as incense. 'As above, so below' is the Hermetic formula explaining our world of appearances. Just as Native American smoke signals carried messages across great distances, aromatic smoke can transmit signals and images between the inner worlds.

The shamanic tradition of the Native Americans also understands this truth and uses sacred pipe smoking to establish good connection and seal the transmission of sacred information. For these purposes the shamans have their own very particular *Kinnikinnik* mixture of herbs.

There is a special fascination in burning a single and pure natural plant substance alone. It allows us to come into contact with an individual plant's personality and experience our own specific reactions to the characteristics of its fragrance. Every aromatic plant expresses its own personality as an intrinsic message in its essential oil. The fragrance released when plants are burned is largely created by these essential oils. They are the means of communication in the plant world.

Fragrance triggers an emotional reaction. We have a special relationship with whatever it is that appeals to us and in turn this has a supportive effect upon us. And in this is revealed the most important tool in discovering which incense to use: our sense of smell. So experimenting with our individual impressions we can develop our very own personal approach. Based on these experiences we now also have the possibility of playing with the dynamics of complementary combinations.

In this way we can attain true understanding that makes burning incense so valuable: self-awareness. We require very little outside training for this. The most significant step is to be true to our own experience and probe what is being triggered within. The only aspect that needs to be learned is how to use the incense and how to select the method.

In order to burn incense in a practical way we can choose from two basic methods. They are described in the following section with all their pros and cons.

Incense tong with charcoal

Burning Incense on Glowing Pieces of Charcoal

The classic way to get incense to smolder away is to scatter it onto small glowing pieces of charcoal in a crucible.

Since it is not so easy to light pieces of charcoal and not everyone has a fireplace, small quick lighting charcoal briquettes have been introduced. The standard briquette has a diameter of 1 to 1.5 inches and has a depression in the middle. As soon as the charcoal starts glowing the incense is placed into this depression.

It is best to pick up the tablet with metal tongs and hold it over a candle flame. The quick lighting effect is due to a mix of compressed charcoal dust with potassium nitrate. This allows the briquette to light immediately and burn on its own as long as there is an adequate supply of air. Blowing on the briquette accelerates the process. After maybe 3–5 minutes it is ready and will have a whitish surface in the light or glow red in the dark.

Charcoal however does have the disadvantage of developing a certain smell of its own when it burns, similar to a sparkler, which some people find disturbing. Placed in an incense container, substances can be burned on the glowing tablet for about 40 minutes before it loses strength and goes out. The briquettes usually come in packets of ten, sealed in an airtight moisture proof roll. Since charcoal attracts moisture, open rolls must always be carefully sealed and kept dry so that they will continue to light easily.

Incense burners

The Incense Burners

A few things are necessary in a functional incense burner. Firstly check that the substantial heat that develops in the smoldering briquette is shielded underneath and does not scorch table it rests on. At the same time a good supply of oxygen is indispensable for the incense to burn evenly and completely.

Clay incense burner filled with sand

Modern incense bowls with perforated tin insert

Hence antique incense burners often sport a perforated rim that protects the surroundings yet still allows the air to flow.

A burner like the one illustrated above is filled two-thirds with sand. It's a good idea to make furrows in the sand (for example using a fork) positioning the charcoal in such a way that air for the burning is available also from below. This guarantees the briquette will be completely consumed.

A more modern apparatus is a burner with a perforated tin insert. This is the optimal solution for ventilating the glowing briquette. It allows the heat to be shielded downside by a cushion of air. You can also carry the burner about between thumb and index finger without burning yourself, thanks to the extended top.

It's a lovely surprise at a garden party to fill a large crucible with glowing coals from the barbecue and have it burn aromatic woods, herbs and resins with their enchanting fragrance. You charge the entire atmosphere with magic and also maybe ward off plagues of pesky insects.

Burning Incense on a Stainless Steel Sieve

Growing demand for a somewhat *cleaner* way to burn incense has recently produced a process which is borrowed from aromatherapy and its familiar fragrance lamps.

Aromatic plant material is burned on a very finely meshed stainless steel sieve about 1 inch above the tip of the flame of a conventional tea candle. In this process the heat can be varied by changing the distance between flame and substance. A very intense and authentic impression of the fragrance is diffused even though less smoke develops. This fine meshed sieve can also be used to burn resins—as long as the principle of 'less is more' is observed.

Olibanum, myrrh, guggul, benzoin, mastic and sandarac can be burned quite easily in this manner. Resins and resinoids that are quite liquid (spruce, elemi) should be burned together with wood or herbs whenever possible because these partially absorb the resin creating a homogeneous combination of fragrances. When extremely liquid incense substances are to be burned on the sieve there is always the last ditch method of placing them on a piece of aluminum foil.

Burning incense on a sieve is an excellent way to experiment with all types of fragrance. For example the ENNEAROM **'Incense Cycle'** in which nine substances are applied in succession is **only** possible using an incense sieve. This way each newly added substance is always completely present in the foreground for about 3 minutes and can be perceived specifically on its own before becoming part of the *supporting background* and integrating with the blend that is already active.

This slow transition and the developing background of a composition that then evenly emits its fragrance over an extended period is a fascinating experience.

The sieve makes it possible to burn incense as a 'parlor game' in which everyone expresses his or her individual impression of each fragrance in a very personal way. The character of each participant emerges clearly showing something of who they are. The composition then constructively accompanies the shared process like an aromatic cloud and becomes a protective shield.

Of course it is important to clean the sieve in order to have a completely neutral starting point the next time it is used. The first step is to press on the bottom side of the cooled sieve causing all of the coarser residue to fall off. The remaining resin can be burned off directly over a flame. The sieve must then be brushed off. Keep on hand a good metal brush for this purpose. The ones used to roughen up suede shoes work well and you can't manage without one. You can buy brushes designed especially for this purpose—at a price!

For practical reasons the sieve has to be made of stainless steel, hence it cannot rust and a bit of detergent will remove all the soot and leave it always looking shiny and new.

The Incense Stove

A useful and decorative burner can be built based on the same principles as the aroma lamp.

The holder for the sieve is placed in such a way that its indentation rests about 1 or 1.5 inches above the tip of the flame. The tea light should sit protected in a vessel made of some fireproof material (ceramic, metal or glass) so that the flame is sure to get enough air. A little sand underneath the tea candle makes it easy to clean quickly in case the wax runs over. It also allows variation in the distance between flame and sieve.

A lid with holes can be another advantage for such a stove because it allows heat to gather underneath the lid protecting the material and causing it to smolder evenly.

Once again, it is worth remembering that an open flame needs to be treated with the greatest attention. Experience has too frequently shown how unpredictable fire can be.

Since many resins and resinoids in particular are very flammable it really is necessary to take a cautious approach and do it safely. Always test the reaction with very small amounts of the material to be used and position the stove on a fireproof surface. Above all never let it burn unattended!

The common paraffin tea light candle is suited to these types of stoves. Burn them in a glass container only and **always** remove the aluminum case! The wick should be standing in the middle of the liquid wax and needs to be checked from time to time. Also don't burn beeswax or stearin candles since these burn at a much higher temperature.

Feathers

To better *sniff* its particular qualities we can fan the rising aromatic smoke. We instinctively know this and often fan smoke toward us with our hands. A feather is perfectly suited to this purpose, *stroking* the air and subtly swirling the fragrance, allowing it to be perceived more intensely. This swirling appears to transmit the fragrance more clearly. Even the untrained observer will immediately feel his senses resonating with it.

Mixing and Composing

It is basically possible to mix together any aromatic substances in order to develop special compositions and recipes. As in cooking, sky is the limit for creativity here.

In specialized literature on this topic we frequently find particular combinations intended for certain effects and for special occasions. These recommendations usually have traditional or spiritual origins.

Astrology, occultism and ethnic shamanistic conventions are fertile fields that have popped up many of these recipes. They seek to encourage the reader to accept a prescribed experience. Not disputing this, the chapter on the individual incense substances does contain information on their traditional backgrounds.

My particular preference however is to try to help strengthen the competence of the individual and ignite their creative power. The best possible outcome is for personal experience to be the guide. Intui-

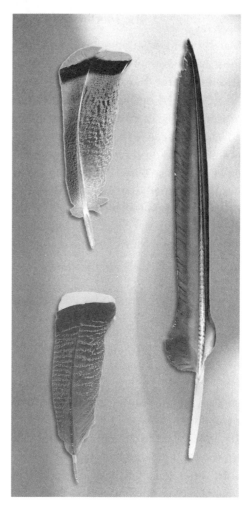

tion plays such an important role in this because it is the voice of the heart that wants to be heard.

Use your nose to guide you to find exactly what is right for *you* at any given moment. A *cookbook* may of course provide useful stimulation. And, as such, recipes like the fragmentary one for traditional Ancient Egyptian *kyphi* are excellent if they arouse in you desire to do your own experimenting.

The Mortar and Pestle

Many of the incense materials available on the market have not been fully processed. This means that they can be cut up more finely, crushed or ground until they are powdered or in a paste-like form. It's an advantage because the aromatic properties are better preserved in this way. For creative incense enthusiasts a mortar and pestle is indispensable for completing the final stages of preparation.

This is delightful work. While pounding in the mortar with the pestle the aromas unfold so wonderfully as to bring us inspiration while we work. And we find ourselves readily engaging in an inner dialog with the plant itself, which is after all the main contribution to a successful end product.

Kyphi

As mentioned earlier this is the famous incense from Ancient Egypt. It was a main export in that era and its composition has been handed down to us on fragments of papyrus and stone tablets from the pyramids.

It was said to contain, among other things, the following substances: myrrh, cardamom, galangal, mastic, cinnamon, benzoin, rose flowers, lemon grass, calamus root, juniper, frankincense and sandalwood.

It is interesting to note that the culinary delights derived from special exotic spices can be reapplied here. The senses are also inspired when these are burned. For example sultanas can be soaked in red wine overnight for preparation of *kyphi*. Individual ingredients should be pounded in the mortar and kneaded well with the mashed sultanas and a tiny bit of wild honey. The paste is then rubbed between the palms of the hands and spread on a cloth to dry for several days in a dark, cool airy place.

When a mixture created in this way is burned it will spread a sweet aromatic fragrance that is extremely relaxing. Burned in the evening it is said to chase away all the worries of the day.

Dried prunes are used in the Japanese world of exotic incense and many other dried fruits also lend themselves as possible aromatic components. Classic binders like those already mentioned in the production of incense sticks are tragacanth and gum arabic which are stirred to a thick mucilage with water. The prepared substances are then mixed in and blended into a pliable paste that firms up nicely after it has dried.

Clearly there is a vast experimental canvas awaiting the creative incense burning artist.

Incense Burning Rituals

A ritual is a purposeful activity that seeks to emphasize a certain intention. Symbolism of objects, words, images and signs supports the action and reinforces the intention leading to a deeper connection between our interiority and the outside world. In rituals aromatic smoke lends a very special power.

What type of purpose can such a ritual fulfill? Simply answered, it is to

lead people back into the inner circle of life.

To remain outside this circle means alienation, separation and isolation from the community of the living. Loneliness, mistrust, rejection and fear are its consequences and these are *not* healing elements. Healing is everything that leads to an inner connectedness with life. This is the holistic approach to health and well-being and also corresponds to the shamanic vision of the world. The holistic approach to life is receiving increasingly more attention in Western cultures.

In the shamanic sense healing means integration or reintegration into the community of life. No aspect is meaningful apart from its interplay with the great whole. The value of such rituals can always be measured by the extent to which they serve the life process and support its development.

In other words incense rituals are a tool with which we approach a situation that we consider desirable from a holistic point of view.

Since symbolism plays a significant part in the practice of rituals it is advisable to take a close look at the language of signs and symbols.

Whenever our everyday language is inadequate such that something inexpressible arises, we seek signs and images to express the phenomenon. These signs or images then come to represent meaningful content without having to be put into words.

It is important always to perceive a ritual as an activity that brings us into the present moment. What is significant is not that which happened yesterday or will happen tomorrow but only what is going on in the present moment, the here and now. Once we center ourselves in the present we then have the freedom to create our own rituals, or own lives. We do not need to resort to traditional forms where we imagine there is more truth than there is right here, right now in ourselves.

Ultimately, we only do that because we are under the illusion that the past is separate from the present and thus more important. In the space of the present lies all authenticity hence we can create our own rituals from within.

With this understanding here is a series of suggestions for rituals that may serve as inspiration. There is a symbol illustrated on this leaf of the Pipal or Bodhi tree (Ficus religiosa). This mighty tree has great religious significance and is one of the most important holy trees in Indian mythology. Its leaves are used in ritual worship as an offering to request a happy relationship between two people.

The Bodhi tree represents the masculine principle and is said to give women the gift of fertility. According to superstition Lakshmi, the Goddess of Happiness and Prosperity resides within this tree particularly on Sundays. According to the Hindu religion the Pipal supports all wishes brought to it in a reverent manner especially when accompanied by a smoke offering.

Buddhist literature holds that Gautama sat meditating in enlightened ecstasy for seven days beneath this tree as he looked to the East with heartfelt desire for perfect knowledge and all-embracing wisdom.

A new understanding of the connectedness of all individual existence was revealed to him. The fateful power of existence born in ignorance throws its shadow on all manifesting souls in their unquenchable thirst for life. He thereby recognized the eternal cycle of creation, suffering and decay, of death and rebirth. This is why this tree is also called the *Tree of Enlightenment*—the Bodhi Tree. It has deep and strong roots. Its trunk embodies the connection between the visible and the

invisible worlds, and its branches and roots represent striving for perfection.

It is said that no lie can remain undiscovered under this tree, which is also called the Tree of Justice. In various parts of India court is held beneath a Pipal tree.

In Nepal the Pipal is looked on as a bridge between heaven and earth upon which souls of the virtuous may rest and revive on their way. In India the leaves are painted with religious motifs to intensify devotional prayer.

Each of the following rituals is associated with a symbolic motif from one of the various cultures around the world and resonates with the particular topic.

So let each symbol stimulate your imagination and watch carefully to see what associations arise for you and which emotions they evoke.

The substances that are suggested for each ritual have been selected on the basis of the Ennearom system. It works well to burn them one after another, but it is also interesting to make up your own mixture or even develop your own personal recipes.

The chapter on **'Outlines of the Incense Substances'** (see page 68) contains descriptions of the plants and their components. Take a close look at these and allow its effect on you if you feel that one of the rituals is especially appealing. Ponder your intentions. What could lie behind this ritual for you? At times this may even trigger a true burst of creativity. Remember: Every creative impulse supports your intention and will intensify the power of the ritual!

Cleansing

and

Clearing

The Light Source Behind the Darkness

This theme embraces everything that may be described as the transformation of disturbed special energy. The area that we physically occupy, be it our home or somewhere that we temporarily wish to use fulfills an essential function. It should be a place of retreat, protection, intimacy, sleep, love and joy. It is a space that should nourish us. In the best case it should be our place in the sun.

In order to engender this state it is worth exploring the many possibilities offered by burning incense. Basically what we are striving for in attempting to transform disruptive influences is to activate the source of light behind the darkness. Nothing happens in a vacuum. Problems that we face have a special reason for presenting themselves and are directly related to us.

Aggression, Illness and Death

A room in which someone has suffered or experienced a difficult death may continue to *exhale* this intense process for a long time afterwards. Resistance to reality has manifested itself so strongly that the associated oppression lingers on. It is like the swinging of the pendulum of a large and heavy clock. With intensive use of incense we can accelerate the dissipation of this energy. It lightens the heaviness and brings relief and refinement. The repulsion that is created by the heaviness dissolves in the air and in love.

Vehement aggression also leaves behind atmospheric disturbances in a room. They too can be dissolved in this way and made to vanish. It is simply energy hiding the sunshine like invisible clouds which may now disperse.

Suggested Incense Substances

1. Dragon blood (Daemenorops draco)
2. Camphor (Cinnamomum camphora)
3. Sage (Salvia officinalis)
4. Cedar wood (Juniperus virginiana)
5. Juniper berries (Juniperus communis)
6. Copal (Protium copal)
7. Asafoetida (Ferula asa foetida)
8. Rosemary (Rosemarinus officinalis)
9. Frankincense (Boswellia carteri)

Preparation and Selection of the Incense Substances

With the exception of asafoetida which has a very pungent garlic like smell all of the suggested ingredients are also well suited for burning individually. But it is a good idea also to prepare an incense mix. While focusing on the process of preparation this is an excellent opportunity to add your intent to the 'remedy' which you want to use for cleansing. When nine parts make up the whole, the composition can be put together according to your own intuition from these nine parts. Your intuition should always be your guide. Trust your inner voice.

Cleansing and Clearing—the Ritual

First spend some time attuning yourself to your intent. Look for a suitable spot in the room to be cleansed where you can safely place the incense container and prepare this area. The container symbolically represents the fire element. You can add for example a stone for **earth**, a shell or a leaf for **water** and a feather for **air**.

Before lighting the fire you can mentally formulate the purpose of this ritual. Since an intention should be fundamentally constructive and life affirmative it is always useful to find a positive way to express it. Instead of focusing on the residual disruptive energy, we concentrate on attaining the desired condition. No matter what the origin of the disturbance, wishing peace and unburdening to everyone concerned thereby accelerates the release. Try to soothe aggressive vibrations and counter any threats by trusting in the guidance of the forces of light. Your motivation should be the desire for life, love, happiness and joy. Let there be no doubt about this.

Light the fire only once you are filled with this objective. When the fire has started glowing place the incense on it and bless it with the earth symbol. As smoke rises take the water symbol and bless the smoke with that. Connect this mentally with an invitation to the elemental forces to support your action.

Now take the feather and the container and bless the air and the fire. Move once in a clockwise direction around the entire room imagining the unfolding of life to be like a river flowing back to the sea. As you do this fan the feather in all directions. Finally walk around the room once more, this time anticlockwise, aware that your intent may strongly influence the current of life. Let it flow freely.

Then you can set the container down, leave the room, close the door and allow the process to take effect for some two to three hours. Later, open the windows and doors to allow all of the energies to escape. Now the room is neutral, clean and pure.

Sensuality

and

Eroticism

The Desire for Partnership
and the Joys of Love

Sensual pleasure and the enjoyment of satisfying desire are splendid privileges of human beings, the wonder of which is especially revealed when they are celebrated with subtle sensitivity.

We very much miss this side of life when there is no partner in sight. At such a time he or she must be called into our life. A ritual for strengthening this call is therefore recommended to those wishing for relationship and the joys of love. A certain resonance effect occurs when the image of a desired state is created and put out into the cosmos. Burning incense is a fine way to help carry such prayers and wishes over the threshold of the third into the fourth dimension. According to the laws of attraction such a message will find the appropriate recipient and the contact will manifest sooner if not later.

Within a relationship a ritual may be invoked as preparation for a beautiful evening of love. In the Old Testament (*Song of Solomon*) King Solomon who adoringly describes the Queen of Sheba's charms in terms of aromatic plant fragrances certainly already knew that incense inspires the senses. An incense ritual can definitely deepen emotional intensity and increase sensitivity toward one's partner.

Suggested Incense Substances

1. Cinnamon bark (Cinnamomum cassia)
2. Damiana (Turnera diffusa)
3. Siam benzoin (Styrax tonkinensis)
4. Ginger root (Zingiber officinale)
5. Myrrh (Commiphora abyssinica)
6. Sunset hibiscus seeds (Hibiscus abelmusk)
7. Guaiacum wood (Guajacum officinale)
8. Guggul (Commiphora mukul)
9. Coriander (Coriandrum sativum)

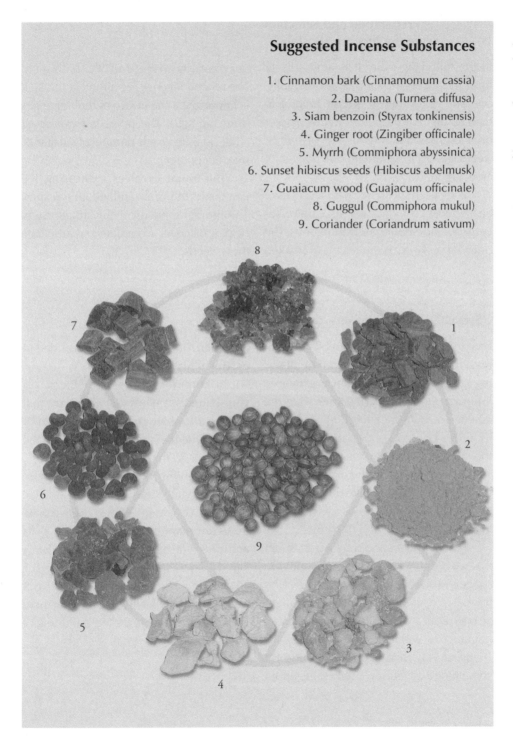

Preparation and Selection of the Incense Substances

In the following ritual it is advisable to burn the incense materials individually, one after the other. It is also helpful to read up on their properties in the chapter on 'Description of the Incense Materials' (see page 13) to stimulate our powers of association.

Since each substance has its very own characteristics it naturally also addresses very specific emotional connotations. The ritual for seeking a partner aims to awaken our creativity on the level of visualization. The related incense are aimed at this so it is important to be aware of their energies from the start. The point is to discover what qualities each particular substance may encourage.

This ritual involves expressing the personal truth of an individual's desires. The aim of the incense in this situation is to help us discover, formulate and articulate these needs.

Sensuality and Eroticism—the Ritual

Prepare a beautiful place to sit. This ritual is performed with the intention of attaining to a greater understanding and deeper intimacy. Honesty and openness are the qualities of such a meeting. Begin this ritual by sitting opposite your partner with the incense stove between you.

One of you places the first incense on the stove. If you would like to, hold hands while one partner expresses a wish related to sensuality, desire and devotion.

No comment should be made about this wish. Let it simply remain within the space and be absorbed in the silence of the fragrance. The other partner then should also express a wish, either with the same fragrance or with the following one.

Next you each express gratitude for something that you very much value about the other. More incense may be added to enhance this gratitude.

In the third stage describe what makes your partner so worthy of your trust that you wish to share this ritual with him or her. Add the remaining substances to the fire as you do this.

Both of you now direct your entire attention within and feel the instinctive needs in your own bodies. Sense how these are manifesting in your very cells and for several minutes remain completely still within this experience.

In conclusion both of you enter your own heart space feeling the longing there and allowing it to guide the unfolding of the rest of the love ritual.

Movement

and

Joy

Maintaining the Physical Body and Its Vital Energy

Plant materials have long been known to help preserve food. The smoke of certain types of wood and herbs has strong preservative and germicidal effects which allow foodstuffs to resist physical decomposition.

Foods high in proteins are often cured to preserve them. It is a method that has roots in every traditional culture.

The *vitality* which may be drawn from physical nourishment is preserved for an extended period of time also in this manner. It is an analogy that can similarly be applied to the preservation of the physical body and its vital energy.

One of the most important tasks of a **human being** is to support the body spiritually as the vehicle for the soul. Plant forces are completely at the service of Creation. One of their tasks is the regulation of imbalanced states. Thus in these ways they serve humankind in both spheres.

When there is a lack of energy or some imbalance that we would like to redress, incense can be burned to achieve this. And the effects can be wonderfully augmented by integrating this burning into a ritual.

The rituals suggested here aim at creating a type of trance energy on the physical plain and sending it to these areas where it is specifically needed.

Suggested Incense Materials

1. Oakmoss (Evernia prunastri)
2. Frankincense (Boswellia sacra)
3. Cardamom (Elettaria cardamomum)
4. Sandarac (Tetraclinis articulata)
5. Juniper tips (Juniperus monosperma)
6. Siam benzoin (Styrax tonkinensis)
7. Galangal (Alpinia officinarum)
8. Mugwort (Artemisia vulgaris)
9. Cedar wood (Juniperus virginiana)

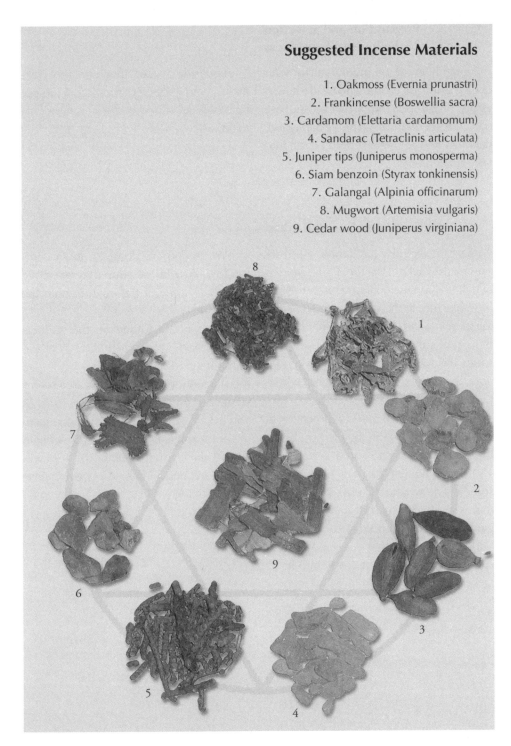

Preparation and Selection
of the Incense Substances

Thoroughly grind the ingredients of your choice using the mortar and pestle if necessary. Break open the cardamom and use only the seeds inside. The cedar wood, oakmoss and galangal should be cut into very small pieces.

Set aside a small pinch each of oakmoss, sandarac, cardamom and juniper tips before you mix the components together.

Movement and Joy—the Ritual

Prepare to exercise or dance. Be fully present as you light the fire. Place a pinch of oakmoss on the coals and with this gift of smoke turn to the cold north. Next add the sandarac and with it symbolically greet the rising sun in the east. Give the hot south the fragrant smoke of cardamom and the juniper tips to the west where the sun sets.

Ask the forces of the four directions to strengthen your vitality before you begin the exercises, which should last at least 15 minutes so that the body experiences some exertion. Select a physical exercise that is familiar to you. It may be dance, gymnastics or hatha yoga perhaps. The important thing is that you enjoy it and can throw yourself completely into it.

When you are done sit down comfortably in front of your incense stove and place some of the mixture onto the coals.

Concentrate totally on the feelings of your body and the breath. Feel the humming and buzzing within while you focus attention on whichever area seems weak. As you inhale draw in strength. As you exhale direct the incoming energy to the point of weakness and let the strength spread throughout your body. This will have a healing influence on your sense of well–being while lending you strength and vitality.

Harmony

and the

Joy of Creativity

Discovering Inner Harmony

When the assorted elements of life are cooperating harmoniously we have an expression of the fertile merging of opposites.

Attaining inner harmony means mastering the dance of opposites. This is however only arrived at through a surrender to change. The results are manifold, delivering abundance and delight at the wonder of being.

When we feel torn between conflicting emotions, alternating between high elation one moment and utter depression the next, we are in conflict with the principles of creation and destruction.

Since the dynamic interplay of these two polarities of life gives rise to fertility, an incense ritual celebrating creativity and change also serves to heal such a state of conflict. Whether expressed as relationship dependency or job-related conflict they always appear to indicate contradictions to our interests and something we are unable to deal with.

Surrender to change teaches us to honor such contradictions as a welcome expression of life's creativity. The following incense ritual seeks to establish harmony with what is.

Suggested Incense Substances

1. Cassia flowers (Cinnamomum cassia)
2. Opoponax (Commiphora erythraea)
3. Tonka bean (Dipteryx odorata)
4. Benzoin sumatra (Styrax benzoin)
5. White sage (Salvia apiana)
6. Cedar tips (Thuja plicata)
7. Lavender (Lavandula officinalis)
8. Frankincense somalia (Boswellia carteri)
9. Rose flowers (Pink damascena)

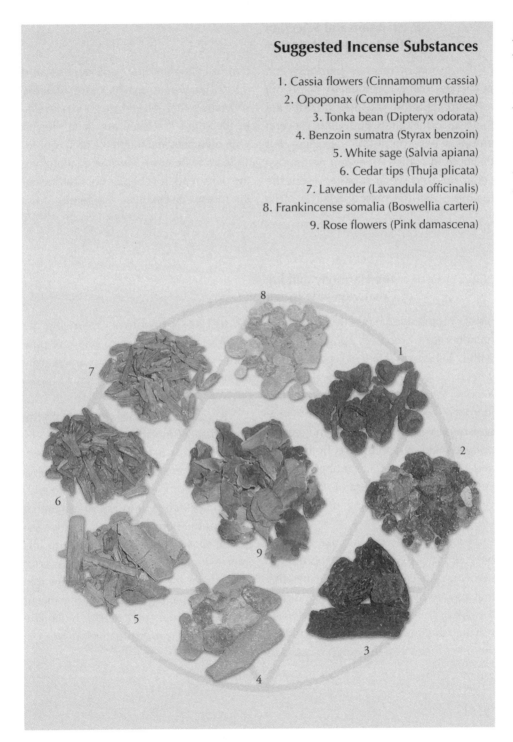

Preparation and Selection
of the Incense Substances

In this group of incense hardness and gentleness come together. Try them out individually before you move on to the actual heart of the rituals. Put together several groups of two contrasting fragrances. For example in Native American mythology cedar tips and white sage represent the feminine and the masculine. The same contrast applies to frankincense and opoponax (sweet myrrh). Categorize the substances that you feel are good partners, in the sense that they are according to your own personal fragrance preferences. To learn to be more sensitive to matching the pairs read the chapter on 'Outlines of the Incense Substances.' (page 68)

The Harmony and Joy
of Creativity—the Ritual

Sit in a comfortable place with your incense paraphernalia prepared. Focus attention within. Where do you feel separation? In what way do you not allow the opposites to come together? Let the conflict play out in front of your inner eye. A problem may consist of: wanting one thing and feeling obliged to do something else, both loving and hating your partner, wanting to be free yet still feeling dependent or valuing life very much while knowing all along that you will have to die.

Experience the conflict like a drama on your inner movie screen. Thoroughly savor one aspect while burning an incense that appears to represent it. Next consider the opposite aspect and really feel your way into this contrary perspective, adding the other incense of the group of pairs to the first as its opponent. Following the first fragrance this second one will now come to the foreground as you inwardly experience the impressions that it triggers for you.

You can repeat this process with the other pairs of incense.

After 3 to 5 minutes you will perceive an aromatic synthesis. Sense how the two fragrances merge and unite with each other. A new impression arises that assumes the perspective of a creative solution. Open yourself completely to this impression since it can whisper to your inner ear an answer from the inexhaustible reservoir of life. The more totally you can surrender to this experience the higher the probability of a truly creative answer.

Meditation

and

Relaxation

AUM as a Symbol
of Universal Oneness

When the hustle and bustle of life's daily current has become so nerve racking that you constantly feel uneasy and out of balance, and you are in the process of getting bogged down then it is high time occasionally yet with clear intent to turn towards silence.

AUM is the symbol of the oneness of the universe, uniting beginning and end. All of life's difficulties pale in the light of the positive energy radiating from this sign. The sound of the spoken syllable, AUM, vibrates as an intensely unifying integrating force leaving stillness and silence in its wake. It is the fertile ground for constructive solutions and new paths.

So when you need to find yourself and wish to create a space within that permits new possibilities, an incense ritual may transform these into reality.

Suggested Incense Substances

1. Vervain (Verbena officinalis)
2. Eucalyptus (Eucalyptus globulus)
3. Sandalwood white (Santalum album)
4. Frankincense (Boswellia serrata)
5. Vetiver (Vetiveria zizianoides)
6. Amber (Succinum)
7. Bay leaves (Laurus nobilis)
8. Angelica root (Angelica archangelica)
9. Copal (Protium copal)

Preparation and Selection
of the Incense Substances

For this ritual it works well to make an 'ideal' meditation mixture from the incense substances listed above. Create the composition as you feel to, either purely intuitively or with the help of a pendulum. Then carefully break up the materials, crush them with a mortar and pestle and mix them well. Preparing them with your own hands allows your intent to flow into the mixture.

Meditation and Relaxation—
the Ritual

Kneel, sitting on your heels or sit in a lotus posture in front of your stove and relax.

Place some of your special mixture on the embers and absorb the fragrance. New space is created when we rid ourselves of the old stuff that has collected. As soon as a disturbing or wandering thought pops up give it to the fire to be transformed along with the plant material. Then once again focus on the fragrance without thinking or wanting anything in particular.

When you have become quite empty and are just filled with the fragrance direct your attention to your heartbeat until you can feel it very clearly. It is a rhythmic vibration that pulsates throughout the entire body.

Stay completely with this physical perception. At the same time start hearing the syllable A-U-M with your inner ear. This sound and the rhythm of your heartbeat will merge with each other and become one. Maintain this state as long as possible. To conclude listen to the echo alone until perfect silence prevails. Deep relaxation and absolute peace will arise. In this silence we are united with the source of all inspiration.

Protection

and

Help

God Experiences the World
Through the Human Eye

To be cared for, to feel protected, simply to be *seen* are profoundly significant human needs. Sometimes life may seem as if we have been abandoned helpless in the wilderness, completely alone. The rule of the game that this illusion puts us at the mercy of seems to be: eat or be eaten. The Fall of Man and his expulsion from Paradise is a fitting image here. After all, this illusion needs to be as convincing as possible since the point is to rise from it and develop our own responsibilities as creative beings.

The ritual of the Egyptian symbol of "Utchat" (the Eye of Horus) is based on the omnipresent protection and presence of the spiritual world from which we can receive help at any time we establish the necessary contact. The decisive factor is our own willingness to perceive this possibility.

Conversely we are *seen* to the extent to which we know ourselves. A spiritual pearl of wisdom says that:

God experiences the world through the human eye.

Consequently we find our connection to the divine within ourselves. An incense ritual can quite decidedly promote this access.

Suggested Incense Substances

1. Inula (Inula helenium)
2. Fennel (Foeniculum vulgare)
3. Spruce resin (Picea abies)
4. Dammar (Canarium strictum)
5. Myrtle leaves (Myrtus communis)
6. Sandarac (Tetraclinis articulata)
7. Rosemary (Rosemarinus officinalis)
8. Tolu balsam (Myroxylon balsamum)
9. Star anise (Illicum verum)

Preparation and Selection
of the Incense Substances

It is certainly helpful to try out the suggested substances individually for yourself. Select three of them to burn in this ritual.

Protection and Help—the Ritual

Trust is essential in this ritual. It involves using the present moment to find our own center, since the fundamental trust that flows from there is vital for our sense of 'being cared for'.

"May I be the way I am?"

The ritual should begin with this question.

Feel within to find the congestion.

What situations do you find unpleasant because you don't think you can manage what is expected of you? What do you believe you need to protect yourself from? What are you afraid of?

Take the first incense substance to which you are drawn and place it on the embers or stove. As you do so imagine the fire transforming this issue and the fragrant smoke creating an expression of trust which is now expanding in place of fear. This will have brought you a step closer to your center.

With the next substance focus on the darkness of limited thinking as the fire transforms it into radiance. Feel the lightness in the fragrance as it brings forth stillness and serenity, revealing the illusory nature of what threatens you. This phase will confer security on your center.

The third substance represents your limitations, which, through the aromatic smoke, are transformed into independence and freedom. Let yourself fall into this realization and feel how you become filled with a powerful lightness from which arises a natural and joyful beingness. You *are* connected with the spiritual world from where new energy can be drawn.

Wisdom

and

Healing

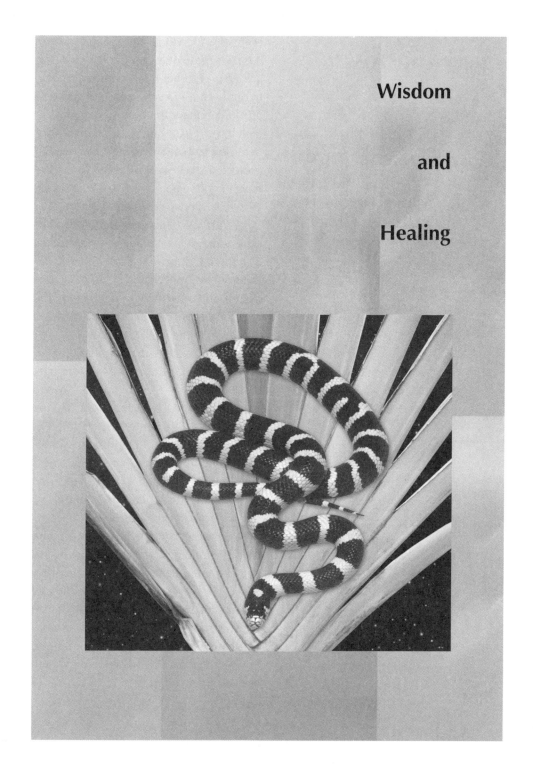

You Are Director
on the Stage of Your Life

For every individual the trauma of birth reenacts the expulsion from Paradise. We are now separate. Over and over again in our lives we feel this sense of lack. We are cold, hungry, thirsty or suffer pain. We develop a great variety of strategies for defense and avoidance, because even our protected space seems unsafe to us. We have forgotten how it was to be part of the whole, in the womb of the *mother*.

When we believe in and accept this state of deprivation it begins to take effect as a mental poison. We fall under its influence and, spellbound by fear, become frozen and increasingly paralyzed. The development of our life is at first impeded and then ultimately blocked.

When I believe that I am not beautiful, rich, intelligent or talented enough, that I am too fat, too unimportant or too weak—just simply incapable of making any change—this is a clear symptom of such poisoning. Depressive states, restlessness or feelings of hopelessness develop. Phantoms of worthlessness and meaninglessness which can lead only to despair control our perception.

The recognition that we ourselves are the director on the stage of our own lives can bring about the reverse of this situation. Wisdom and healing are directly connected. Healing also means taking an optimistic approach to life, understanding that there are plenty of opportunities. So this ritual is aimed at creating a calm and confident attitude towards what is to come.

Suggested Incense Substances

1. Calamus root (Acorus calamus)
2. Pine resin (Pinus sylvestris)
3. Himalayan juniper (Juniperus macropoda)
4. Guggul (Commiphora mukul)
5. Bay leaves (Laurus nobilis)
6. Myrrh (Commiphora abyssinica)
7. Patchouli (Pogostemon patchouli)
8. Mastic (Pistacia lenticus)
9. Sandalwood red (Pterocarpus santalinus)

Preparation and Selection
of the Incense Substances

First use the incense stove to find out which of the suggested substances you like, since you can only open up to what you already accept. Wisdom lies in the recognition that everything is good as it is. Both rejection and open-mindedness are accepted.

Simply listen within and select those substances that appeal to you. You may want to place these in a particular order that promises continuously increasing pleasant feelings. Put the indifferent ones at the beginning and the best at the end.

Wisdom and Healing—the Ritual

Make yourself comfortable and have a feather available to fan the incense fragrances.

To attune yourself to this healing ceremony it is helpful to reflect on the purpose of the power that you desire to produce through this ritual. What thought patterns impede the development of your life energy?

The clearer you are about the constrictions the more clearly you will be able to formulate and express your desire for change.

Also feel into your heart space and find the affliction that corresponds to this constriction. Take several deep breaths. As you exhale feel if there are any tensions or constrictions in your body.

Now think of an affirmation, a supportive and positive statement about yourself. If you have doubts about your self-worth

or capabilities a sentence like this might be an appropriate affirmation:

"I am strong and my contribution is important."

Connect your statement with the first incense substance and place a pinch of it on the stove. Fan the fragrance toward you while letting it merge with the affirmation in your mind. This will nourish and motivate you.

After a few minutes repeat this process with the next incense substance, connect it with further or intensified positive statements about yourself. Continue doing this with all of the substances that you have prepared.

Do not forget to show your love and gratitude toward the plant forces, ending the ritual in silent reflection. The effect of this ritual will soon make itself felt in your daily life.

The Strength

and Courage

to Face Life

Fertile Ground for Phantoms

In each of us lives a shaman, an inner healer who counteracts the influence of undesirable energies. Integrating all levels of experience this inner healer fights off disease.

Illness can be seen as a manifestation of an inability to protect oneself. A willingness to tolerate negativity indicates self-evident weakness. One person may be susceptible to a particular virus—of whatever type—and another may not. The same thing applies to the 'evil eye' voodoo or any other type of black magic spell. This illustrates the relationship between power and fear. Each potentiates the other. It is fertile ground for the phantoms that are formed in this constellation. We can only be dominated by something when we believe in it as a possibility. A trusting inner attitude can present a powerful shield of protection to deflect this type of influence.

So the point is to activate this inner source of strength, our inner healer, through ritual symbolism. We are establishing an essential contact connecting us with the universal light, consequently revealing the shadows of the polarity.

Suggested Incense Substances

1. Nutmeg (Myristica fragrans)
2. Galbanum resinoid (Ferula galbaniflua)
3. Copal (Protium copal)
4. Damiana (Turnera diffusa)
5. Syrian rue (Peganum harmala)
6. Fumaria (Fumaria officinalis)
7. Guaiacum wood (Guajacum officinale)
8. Spruce resin (Picea abies)
9. Gray sage (Artemisia tridentata)

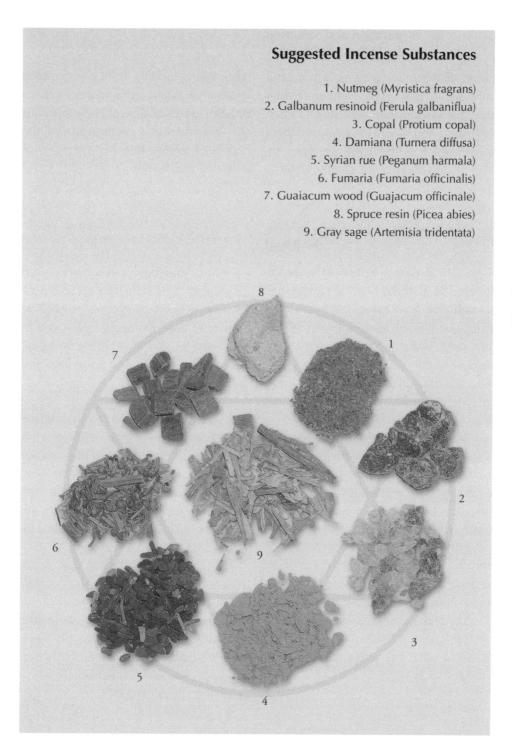

Preparation and Selection
of the Incense Substances

Some of these are extremely powerful substances (gray sage, nutmeg, Syrian rue) that demonstrate very special characteristics. You should definitely test them to see which of them you are open to. This always shows very clearly where a weakness is lurking. The corresponding information is in the chapter on 'Outlines of the Incense Substances'. These materials can be burned in a circle so that all the beneficial aspects become integrated as a defense mechanism.

The Strength and Courage to Face
Life—the Ritual

Take care in preparing the place for the incense ritual. If you like you can arrange a small altar. In all events it is meaningful to include symbols for the four elements of fire, earth, water and air and to ask their respective natures sincerely for support. Visit this ritual place frequently, as it will encourage the development of any qualities that may be lacking.

Select a quality such as courage, strength, endurance, initiative, assertiveness, mindfulness or heartfullness for each substance in line with your personal response to the fragrances. The point is always to discover what will most suitably reestablish the essential connection when the flow of energy appears to be blocked due to some deficiency. The aromatic quality should endeavor to bridge this gap.

Light the incense stove and place the first substance on the sieve while becoming aware of what the nature of this quality means to you.

Close your eyes and focus only on your breathing. Inhale through your nose and then exhale through your mouth. The rhythm of your breathing opens you to your inner world through the flowing air. The missing quality will surge into you with every breath.

After three to five minutes add the next substance and repeat the process with the next quality.

When all of the incense prepared for this round are lying together on the sieve empty yourself completely. Let the light shining in your heart become brighter and brighter until it illuminates your whole inner world.

Let it shine beyond the boundaries of your body. Imagine that this light is radiating out into the entire world.

Stay with this image for a while before, in gratitude, you end the ritual. Change is clearly tangible when a sense of total trust develops. This is the dimension in which your inner healer works.

Energy

and

Transformation

The Stages of Growth

The form of one's being may be altered in a process that has nine steps. Just like the nine months of fetal growth in the mother's womb, there are nine steps of becoming. These are nine aspects that act in a continuous flow with each other and together form one stroke of the pendulum of the great cosmic clock.

When these nine steps are passed through in ritual this symbolically concludes a cycle which energetically creates the impulse for transformation. It can generate dynamic movement when stagnation has become a problem, or precipitate nourishing stillness when hyperactivity has strained the sense of well being. In any case new perspectives become possible in seemingly hopeless conditions.

The Enneagramm symbolizes such a cycle. It is composed of the eternal repeating principle (the periodic Law of Seven) plus the triangle as the principle of the creation of all life. Walking around the circle once symbolically represents the execution of a consummate process allowing it to radiate in all its power. Great vitality can be invoked in this way. It can then be evoked for the most diverse purposes.

Suggested Incense Substances

1. Arbor vitae (Thuja occidentalis)
2. Star anise (Illicum verum)
3. Opoponax (Commiphora erythraea)
4. Sunset hibiscus seeds (Hibiscus abelmusk)
5. Dammar (Canarium strictum)
6. Himalayan juniper (Juniperus macropoda)
7. Rosemary (Rosemarinus officinalis)
8. Frankincense (Boswellia carteri)
9. Sandalwood white (Santalum album)

Preparation and Selection
of the Incense Substances

Arrange all of the nine incense materials as suggested, chronologically in a circle around the little incense stove. Put each one into a small clay bowl or something similar so that it is easy to take a pinch. There are three groups of three substances each: 8/9/1 is the body group, 2/3/4 is the emotion group and 5/6/7 for the mind. If possible have a feather available to fan the smoke and keep a pencil and paper handy to make notes. During the ritual all nine substances will go onto the stove one at a time. Notice how each newly added aroma comes to the foreground completely alone for about 3 minutes before it integrates into the symphony.

Energy and Transformation—
the Ritual

This ritual is wonderful performed alone but it also works for two or more people together. Light the candle in the incense stove with ceremony and close your eyes for a moment to gather your attention.

When you place the first incense of the body group on the stove focus completely on your body and its reactions. If you are alone try to summarize your reaction in a single concept or two to three words that you may want to jot down. In a group situation each person in the circle takes a turn expressing his or her impression of the fragrance. Any type of association is encouraged and everyone else in the group listens respectfully without comment.

Frankincense, the incense with the deepest history in human culture is derived from a hostile environment of the most extreme heat and sunlight. Individual reactions to it can be quite controversial.

Then add the second incense. **Sandalwood**, popular worldwide for its balsamic fragrance and enticing character, it quickly adapts and sneaks into every combination maintaining its background effect. However we may also feel how grounding and centering its masculine steadfastness can be.

Arbor vitae follows as the third substance. Serious and dark it appears with severity and demands clarity. Here is an admonishing voice pleading for critical attention and thriftiness towards resources.

As described, one's personal resonance to these fragrances should be gathered as each one is added. Once all of the body incenses have been placed on the fire like this imagine that these three represent the power and assertiveness of the self. They allow you to perceive the way in which you occupy your own space. As a whole, how has the experience of the impressions caused by the fragrances on the physical level been? Was it rather difficult or was it simply a positive sensation?

Now before you go to the level of the heart be quiet for a moment and look into what you *feel*.

Star anise is the next substance for the stove. The sweet smell that so enticingly beguiles the inner child unfolds its comforting strength as long as mistrust does not cause it to cut itself off. Let yourself go if you can. If not, what do you feel?

Then follows **opoponax,** also known as *fragrant myrrh*. Its balancing, harmonizing elegance enlivens the feminine element, calling on fertility and healing as well as enhancement of the senses.

Sunset hibiscus seeds will now lead you into the catacombs of desire. With its dark unfathomable veil the fragrance of this incense creates a mood both fascinating and at the same time precarious.

Gather your impressions and focus on merging, partnership and opening the heart for which these fragrances are a key. How open you are for the energetic impulses of this level of experience is measured by your receptivity to the fragrances.

Before you continue to the third part, the mental level, concentrate on the stillness within you.

Focus your attention above the bridge of your nose at the 'third eye' and place the **dammar** on the stove. The luminous, bright glow of this fragrance spreads extremely quickly. With lightness and great subtlety it allows thought to fly as it opens the mental gates.

As the next fragrance, the **Himalayan juniper**, unfolds its sublime presence devote yourself reverently to the impression and accept the spiritual guidance that this strong force offers.

The versatility of **rosemary** now brings this ritual to a close. The cheerful life affirming radiance of its aroma will allow an optimistic conclusion with many new possibilities coming into view.

Once again notice your responses, drawing conclusions about your mental tendencies if you can. How open are you to the fragrances on this plane?

The circle for us individually as well as for the group is now complete. While perceiving the fragrant consequences of this ritual thank the forces that have manifested for you. From now on you will be available to many different ways of working on yourself, and it will become easier for you to actually do what you know is important for yourself.

Outlines of the Incense Substance
The Various Planes of Perception for Incense

This description of the aromatic resins, woods, roots, herbs, seeds, leaves and flowers is intended as a guide to establishing mental contact with the world of incense fragrance. This section includes the material phenotypes of the plant substances, botanical facts on aromatic plants, traditional contexts in which they have been used in specific cultures as well as personal individual fragrance impressions, images, ideas and suggested applications.

As an overall impression this information is intended to provide you with a portrait of the incense substances which you may then supplement with your own essential sensory experiences.

Guidelines for Focusing Attention When Burning Incense

If you are searching for a specific incense you will find the most frequently used references in an alphabetical list which follows the descriptive section.

The appendix contains a register where the plant species are organized according to their botanical names. In addition there is a classification of substances according to keywords from traditional use, and a register of the fragrance messages arranged according to elemental forces. This will also allow you to make your selections according to perceptive emphasis and fragrance message.

The Four Elemental Forces

The aromatic plants are classified by color according to the four elements, fire, earth, water and air.

The motif in the margin of the page indicates which elemental force has the primary spiritual effect. The basic structure of this classification is adapted from Martin Henglein's 'Archetypal Fragrance Circle'. So if there is an issue you are working on for which you would like to seek out the elemental force of a particular plant you should first of all decide on which elemental plane you would like to ask for assistance.

The Archetypal Circle of Fragrances corresponds to the cycle of the seasons as they determine the development of life in the plant world. In the time of Spring-like awakening root and sprout are extending into the biosphere (fire). With blossom time comes the highest possible communication and pollination, it is summer and we have the sun at apogee (air).

As the sun sinks lower in the sky and fruit ripen it is harvest time, the time of abundance and the beauty of autumn (water). Preparation for winter follows as the plant world retreats into the earth and into sleep (earth).

The elemental forces that rule each aromatic plant also have an influence on the well being of humans. Our sensory response to these very characteristics is an authentic indication of the extent to which we are able to live with this particular elemental force. We should always be open to an inner dialog with a fragrance, trying to establish just how it makes us feel.

Fire

Fire represents the initiating, igniting energy that sets processes in motion and often forces change. Transformational processes receive, so to speak, ignition through the impulse of fire. Where something seeks to develop, fire sets things in motion. Where stagnation and damp heaviness prevail the fiery energy of a fragrance can create the necessary balance—provided that you are open to it.

So if you are seeking such a balance look to the fiery substances to which you can most clearly relate. It could provide the dynamic impulse for you to expand (yang). The clearest signal for you is whether or not you like the fragrance. If you don't like it there is resistance to its characteristics and it won't be integrated. In this case it should not be forced.

Earth

Earth stands for the preservation and stability of all that exists. Earth energy provides structure and forms the supportive base for all of the possibilities of development in life. It offers life the opportunity to maintain itself. Preparing the soil in which seeds can sprout means living the earth energy. Growing roots and building substance are activities of the warm, dark forces of the earth. If you wish to promote this force look among the earthy substances for those whose fragrance take your heart by storm. Since our current age is so out of touch with reality getting grounded is extremely important for many people. Aromatic plants can be outstanding guides in this respect, because the symbolism of being earthed finds such a strong expression through fragrance. Protective and strengthening, the earth represents qualities ranging from seriousness to severity.

Water

Water is the womb of our secret unconscious life. Our biosphere is born of water. The motherly, nourishing, flowing energy of this element with its wondrous secrets can sometimes also bewilder our senses. It is a creative energy that pulsates with its own innate rhythmic yin force.

Sensitive artistry with its ear close to the heart of things are borne on this watery force. The sweet, extravagant and seductive aromatic fragrances related to this elemental force tell us of the beauty of life and teach us about surrender.

The fruits of existence are formed here. Trusting in the power of water without fear, and immersing ourselves in it is of great significance in our attitude toward ourselves, as it is for our inner healing. The relaxing, harmoniously balancing effect of 'watery' fragrances can help us feel what is going on within our own heart.

Air

Air is the element of fast movement and flexibility. What is one way this moment may be different the next. Air is also the element of communication and multiplicity.

Whatever is luminous, bright, transparent or subtly spiritual belongs to the airy elemental force. Where solutions are found and thoughts are lent wings this force prevails. Airy aromatic plants primarily have an illuminating, mentally stimulating and refreshing quality. These substances are also the ones whose help makes for easier access to the subtle planes. They support clairvoyance but also are quite capable of spacing us out if we are not grounded. On the other hand they will occasionally work wonders in cases of melancholy and depression. So it is always worth searching for what is the most suitable fragrance to expand awareness. This also means attaining to a vision that creates new horizons in our life.

The Three Centers of Perception

Our experience of life is always via one of our three 'centers' or levels of perception: the mind, the emotions and the body. They are characterized by very specific qualities.

Unfortunately we are rarely clearly conscious of which center is perceiving or reacting. Something like an *automatic mechanism* is triggered that all too frequently just leads us into a dead end or up a garden path. In the process suppressed wounds from the past collide with concrete beliefs about the future so that no space is left for the *present*.

If we believe that we are helpful and good, or responsible for everything but 'do good' for fear that the outside world would otherwise let us fall then we are acting out of compulsion yet unaware of it. Our feelings of pride, self-righteousness and arrogance are directly related to this 'illusion'. As a consequence we have put ourselves constantly under pressure.

Then when the body ultimately develops symptoms of exhaustion, indicating that it is at the end of its tether, we don't see this connection either and perhaps even get into artificial stimulants in order to be able to continue in the rat race. All this precedes a state of collapse. Far too many people live like this.

When we become more conscious of our own perceptions, more authentic decisions and actions are available to us in the moment. This enables us to do whatever is needed. And in actual fact it is this state of refined perception in the moment that grants us freedom: Freedom from unrecognized fears that actually dissolve when the light of conscious perception and recognition falls on them. These fears are phantoms of the shadowlands of the mind and are nourished in unconsciousness. They cannot stand up to the light of conscious recognition.

When the three centers of our perception exist in a consciously guided dynamic relationship with each other we become capable of mastering every situation in life.

Mind

Mind is the abode of the concepts, beliefs and ideas that we have about things. Dogmas and convictions that things are as they are and not any other way reside in this center. The limiting aspects of this center become active when we do not recognize that our mental activity is an obstacle to a freely flowing life.

Convictions that are born of fear stand out because they paralyze us in a stance of defensiveness. Anything that we don't acknowledge keeps us imprisoned. The belief that aggression can only be overcome by even greater aggression is fed by anger and itself keeps alive the spiral of violence.

The energetic connection between the mental and the emotional centers is thus clearly demonstrated. Emotions are largely driven by mental activity and in turn empower *these*. When this occurs automatically we are operating at the lower level of the mental center. The fixations located here cause us to reject and criticize, glorify, boast and dramatize. They make us arrogant or egocentric and have us respond in a domineering or even disinterested manner without our having any other choice. We are on preprogrammed automatic.

On the other hand an abundance of possibilities and solutions, the phenomenon of infinite multiplicity exist at the higher mental levels, from where we make our truly free decisions. So it becomes important to nourish thoughts that lead us to the higher and most beautiful possibility of fully realizing our potential.

The mind center bestows the possibility of vision. Through contemplation and meditation, prayer or kriya yoga it is possible to achieve a direct communion with it. Processes to cleanse negative and destructive beliefs, calm the flood of thoughts and prepare for something new as well as to contact the subtle sources can be supported on this plane through impulses garnered from aromatic fragrances.

Opening, rejuvenating and strengthening the mental forces, as well as everything that affects mental dynamics, is directly related to this center. Generally speaking it is slow to react to outside influences and may be regarded as the gateway to all-embracing consciousness.

Emotion

The emotional center is characterized by capriciousness. 'Relationship' is the keyword around which everything in this region revolves. Emotion is defined via the 'other', by the way and degree to which we resonate with the other. On the emotional level the melting together of opposites and YIN, as the internalizing force, determine the polarities.

A creative act is born out of the feminine and the masculine elements uniting at the emotional center. The forces of *attraction* are the energy at work. This means that all elements of attraction, seduction and even manipulation are at home here.

Eroticism, a sense of security, including everything that resonates with the question: "should I be open to this?" belong to this realm. Accordingly the capacity for surrender and shame are the criteria that set the course. Allowing oneself to feel always means taking a risk. We do not *know* where the journey will take us.

Thus we recognize that *trust* plays a large role in this center. Drama begins when trust is lost. It may be experienced as a fall into the abyss or as slowly sinking into a swamp. Fear then transforms into anger or despair, consequently reinforcing negative beliefs about life and feeds destructive mental convictions.

The lower emotional areas are in this way dominated by reflex passions like rage, pride, deception, envy, fear, insatiability, uncontrolled desire and indifference. Since these impulses are faster than those of the mental center they easily take over.

Yet the emotional plane is also directly connected with the soul. The language of the soul can only be understood in this center. The divine opens to us when we perceive the expressions of our emotions consciously, tuning into the language of our soul instead of reactively feeding them with destructive thoughts. Gospel music, devotion and bhava yoga are related to this center as heart opening exercises.

Cleansing the heart is also the most important goal in the *Dhikr* of the Sufis. Fragrances whose essences especially connect with this center are characterized by their soft, support and a rather soothing, relaxing effect. Whatever creates serenity, caresses our senses or awakens sensuality illumines the potentialities of this center. It is the gateway to omnipresent **Love**.

Body

The body is an expression of material reality. We are born into a physical reality that confronts us with the concrete circumstances of time and space. In this field of experience reality on the one hand unfolds very slowly yet it has the fastest reactions of all three centers.

On the material level contradictory tendencies dominate without restraint. Survival involves the need for boundaries and resistance. Here the power of the ego comes to the fore. When destructive thoughts fed by repressed emotions have obstructed the natural flow of life too long the body, as loyal servant, will express this through symptoms of disease.

In the case of sudden danger instinct, which is normally one of the body's subordinate authorities, takes control and causes it to react without allowing the emotions, let alone the mind to get in the way. All of the independent forces are activated at unbelievable speed to maintain life.

Inconceivable strength becomes available at such times. Only later does horror, pain or anger arise and only in the third phase does the mind *realize* what has actually happened. All of us have experienced this in one way or another.

We can consciously influence mind and emotion as well as our overall well being via the physical plain. For example astonishing results in healing are achieved through physical exercise, body postures, mudras (energy-point stimulation) and hatha yoga.

Fragrances whose primary emphasis is on the physical plane help to restore a balanced awareness allowing us to feel what is going on in the body. The YANG aspect of powerful expansiveness dictates the personal concerns of life. These incense experiences revealing the path of clear decision, guide us how best to deal with current circumstances.

The body is the center of **power** because actions on the physical level have an all encompassing significance.

AMBER

Succinum
Conifer
Syn.: Succinite
Part of plant: Resin
Elemental force: FIRE
Emphasis: MIND

Origin

Resin of coniferous trees is also known as 'Gold of the North' in Europe. It can be anything from 20 and 200 million years old. As fossil material it is especially abundant in the Baltic region. Amber is celebrated throughout the world in jewelry and as a protective stone. It can be found almost everywhere. It exudes from a variety of trees such as pine, cedar, juniper, stone pine, cypress etc, all of which guarantee a continuing supply of incense resins.

Traditional Use

In the Middle Ages amber was burned as incense to relieve kidney stones and epilepsy and to protect against the plague. Up to the modern era it has been used as a medicinal incense to accelerate healing. In Traditional Chinese Medicine burning amber is considered effective against states of fear and insomnia, forgetfulness and cramping. The Greeks and Egyptians connected it to the power of the sun and the Sufis use it as incense to free the heart.

Notes on Burning as Incense

This is a slow burning incense with dark to burnt characteristics. A soul fragrance that sometimes reminds of the smell in ancient tombs. Not suitable for short sessions.
Good in combination with benzoin and cedar wood.

Fragrance Message

Ancient stored sunlight transformed into fragrant smoke can lead to very deep states of inner peace.

'Renewal at the place of origin'

ANGELICA ROOT

Angelica archangelica
Angelica officinalis
Umbellate plant/Apiaceae
Syn.: Longwort, wild angelica
Part of plant: Root
Elemental force: EARTH
Emphasis: EMOTION

Origin

A native of Europe and Siberia this perennial plant is now mainly cultivated in Belgium, Hungary and Germany. Its powerful root supports a thick shaft that can grow up to 3 meters (10 feet) in height. The white umbels spread an intense aromatic fragrance.

Traditional Use

Angelica root has been praised since the dawn of time for its extraordinary healing powers. It is said to have a strengthening and protective effect on the heart, circulation and immune system. It is used to relieve rheumatic and respiratory diseases as well as digestive disorders. It was a component of the medieval cure-all *Theriak*. Folk wisdom sees angelica root as a strong force against black magic and the Chinese value its healing qualities for gynecological disorders using it to promote fertility and sharpness of mind.

Notes on Burning as Incense

A powerful earthy/warm smoke with a sharp basic tone that can provides a mighty orientation shift toward the center. Good component in mixtures used for strengthening the power of the self against fear of life and discouragement.

Fragrance Message

Supportive strength from below that leads to decisiveness and self-confidence.

Walking your own path

ARBOR VITAE

Thuja occidentalis
Cypress plant/Cupressaceae
Syn.: Thuja, white cedar, Western red cedar
Part of plant: Twigs
Elemental force: EARTH
Emphasis: BODY

Origin

An elegant, cone-shaped conifer that grows like a column up to 15 meters (45 feet). It is quite modest in its demands and can live to be 800 years old. The home of this tree is the northeast of North America but nowadays it is also cultivated in Europe, especially in France.

Traditional Use

The slender closed contour of this tree shows its Saturnine character. It is often planted along the boundaries between properties as well as at cemeteries, and is considered a symbol for the limitations life. As such Thuja incense was already used in ancient times which can be deduced from the remains of thuja wood in a coal basin in the tomb of Tutankhamen. It has a strongly tonifying effect.

The smoke also has insect repelling properties.

Notes on Burning as Incense

Thuja is toxic when taken orally but there is no problem burning it as incense. The incense fragrance of the twig tips is woody, dark and serious in its expression. Thuja sternly indicates the essential issues, dealing with the integration of what we deny and do not wish to see.

Fragrance Message

Gets to the point and leads to the meaning of life.

'Concentration on reality'

ASAFOETIDA

Ferula asa-foetida
Umbellate plant/Apiaceae
Syn.: Asfetida
Part of plant: Root
Elemental force: EARTH
Emphasis: MIND

Origin

This large perennial plant is native to Afghanistan, Iran and neighboring regions. It achieves a height of up to 3 meters (10 feet) with yellow widely branched umbels and forms thick fleshy roots.

Traditional Use

Asafoetida is burned by the Tibetan Bön shamans as incense for exorcist healing rituals as 'Holder of the Life Wind' to drive out destructive demons. It is used as a medicinal/ritual incense for mental disorders and also as an aphrodisiac. It is considered the most important incense remedy for magical and miracle treatments.

The Persians use it as potency remedy. As the traditional name already suggests this is purely and simply *the* remedy for warding off devils, ghosts, demons, witches and similar energies. This is not a surprise considering its extreme garlic-like aroma. In Ayurveda it is considered a stimulant for *agni*—digestive fire.

Notes on Burning as Incense

Despite its extreme incense fragrance asafoetida produces an intensely relaxing and sedative effect. Added in very small amounts it brings a grounding note as the soothing quality to a love incense mixture.

Fragrance Message

A polarizing stimulus that unites extremes and makes everything possible.

'At the center of the cyclone'

77

BAY LEAVES

Laurus nobilis
Bay plant/Lauraceae
Syn.: Sweet bay, bayberry, laurel berry, bay laurel
Part of plant: Leaves
Elemental force: AIR
Emphasis: MIND

Origin

This evergreen tree from the Mediterranean area grows to a height of 10 to 20 meters (30 to 60 feet) and is sometimes found in bush form. It has black berries and dark green leaves which contain glands full of essential oil. The male and female flowers grow together as small umbels out of the rachis. In the Canary Islands the bay tree grows in rain forests that filter water from the air like a green lung and channel it down into the soil.

Traditional Use

In addition to their status as a popular kitchen herb, in earlier times the leaves were also used medicinally for gastrointestinal disorders and fever. Bay has a stimulating effect on the lungs, circulation and the lymphatic system. A crown of bay leaves is an ancient symbol of fame and honor. In early Greek times it was burned as incense to cleanse and for fortune telling, and is frequently mentioned in connection with the Oracle of Delphi.

Notes on Burning as Incense

The smoke serves as a bridge between dream and reality. It strengthens self-confidence. Bay can also be used as incense to increase sensual receptivity and to help deal with suppressed issues in the present.

Fragrance Message

Provides mental stimulation and an opening to overcome everything negative through contact with the spiritual self.

'The eyes look ahead with positivity'

BOLDO

Peumus boldus Mol.
Monimia tree, monimiaceae
Syn.: Boldu, Boldotree
Part of plant: Leaves
Elemental force: AIR
Emphasis: MIND

Origin

This evergreen shrub-like tree is a native of the Chilean highlands and attains a height of up to 6 meters (20 feet). It blossoms throughout the entire year and its firm foliage has been harvested for cultic medicinal applications for more than 10,000 years.

Traditional Use

In Chilean and Bolivian folk medicine boldo is an indispensable naturopathic remedy. Whether as a digestive spice in foods, a tincture to relieve rheumatism or venereal disease, a compress for toothache or earache or taken internally for liver and gallbladder disorders the effectiveness of boldo leaves is always trusted by the indigenous people of these areas.

Together with copal, boldo is also burned as incense by the Native Americans for sleep disorders and nervousness. During the colonial period boldo leaves were brought to Europe as a promising medicine for the treatment of venereal disease. According to tradition the leaves were also sometimes burned as incense to alleviate mental disorders.

Notes on Burning as Incense

The dried chopped leaves produce a very pleasant incense spreading a powerful spicy/fruity/sour fragrance which is well suited for brightening, clearing and cleansing rituals.

Fragrance Message

Calm and harmonious atmosphere when the cleansing force has driven away the nerve wracking elements.

'Healing absence of thoughts'

CALAMUS ROOT

Acorus calamus
Calamus aromaticus
Aroid plant/Araceae
Syn.: Flagroot
Sanskrit: *vasha ('power of the word')*
Part of plant: Root
Elemental force: WATER
Emphasis: EMOTION

Origin

A native of India and Burma this reed-like swamp plant with its sword shaped leaves grows on the banks of lakes and rivers. It is similar to the iris and forms a horizontal root system that is up to 1 meter (3 feet) in length pushing its fleshy tubers down into the mud. Since the 16th Century it has also been known in Europe and North America.

Traditional Use

In India the plant is considered a folk remedy for digestive disorders, headaches and coughs. In Egypt the root is taken as an aphrodisiac. It is associated with Venus and used to treat gynecological disorders. In the Himalayas this incense is burned as a mind-brightening tonic for the nerves during meditation. Powers of mental revitalization have been ascribed to it and Native Americans (Cheyenne) value the cleansing strength of calamus incense during sweatlodge ceremonies.

Notes on Burning as Incense

The woody/leathery oriental fragrance tone is outstanding when blended into a mixture and combines together the sensual and the spiritual.

Fragrance Message

A gentle magical mood arises and allows new trust in our own expressiveness to develop.

'Allowing sensitive perception'

CAMPHOR

Cinnamomum camphora
Bay plant/Lauraceae
Syn.: Chin. dragonbrain
Part of plant: Resin crystal
Elemental force: FIRE
Emphasis: BODY

Origin

The mighty evergreen camphor tree is a native of south- east Asia. It grows with gnarled branches, attains a height of up to 50 meters (150 feet) and can achieve a diameter 5 meters (15 feet). It bears small green/yellow/whitish fascicles of flowers that give red berries. After the age of about 50 years it begins to exude the crystalline raw camphor, which is also distilled from mature wood.

Traditional Use

In the Himalayas camphor is called the "medicine of the wild man" which may even be a reference to the Yeti. It increases *prana* and simultaneously opens the senses. In Indian mythology camphor is associated with Shiva, the God of Intoxication and Eroticism, even though it has a subduing effect on sexual energy. It possesses the moon's watery element in a field of tension with fiery initiative.

Ayurveda uses it as a sedative to treat hysteria and nervousness. But it also has a stimulating effect in depressive states and relieves muscle tension, strengthens the action of the heart, the circulation and the entire autonomic nervous system. It is both hot and cold at the same time. Camphor is a component of many insecticides.

Notes on Burning as Incense

In no case should camphor be taken internally. White crystalline camphor is highly flammable and great care must be taken when burning it as incense. The smoke is fast and intense. It is penetrating, clarifying, fresh and fades away very quickly. Do not burn this incense in the presence of babies and small children!

Fragrance Message

The ability to concentrate with consciousness creates clarity.

'Stepping forward and being strong'

CARDAMOM

Elettaria cardamomum
Ginger plant/Zingiberaceae
Part of plant: Fruit
Elemental force: FIRE
Emphasis: EMOTION

Origin

A native of tropical Asia this reedy perennial is also cultivated in Central America nowadays. With a root system that creeps on the ground it produces reed-like leaf stems of 4 and sometimes even 5 meters tall (12 to 15 feet) and panicles of yellowish flowers with purple tips develop from separate somewhat smaller shoots. Green to whitish seed capsules are formed from these flowers, each containing three locules with 5 to 6 aromatic seeds inside.

Traditional Use

A kitchen spice that promotes digestion, cardamom flavors a great variety of gourmet foods and even medications. It is also used as a fragrance in soaps, cosmetics and perfumes. As a traditional medicine in China and India it has been known for 3,000 years as an effective remedy for lung disease, digestive problems, fever, urinary complaints and nervous disorders as well as a treatment for poisonous bites and insect stings. In addition it has always been used as an incense in India as it was in ancient Egypt.

Notes on Burning as Incense

The sensual tonifying and nerve balancing effect of cardamom incense can bring us encouragement in difficult situations or states of exhaustion. It generates movement.

Fragrance Message

The principle of hope where a solution can always be found when we have a positive basic attitude.

'Confidence and joy in life'

CASSIA FLOWERS

Cinnamomum cassia
Cinnamomum aromaticum nees
Bay plant/lauraceae
Syn.: Chinese cinnamon
Part of plant: Buds
Elemental force: FIRE
Emphasis: EMOTION

Origin

This slender evergreen tree is a native of south-western China where it is cultivated commercially as a cropped shrub. It can also be found in Vietnam and India. The dried flower buds have a diameter of 3–5 mm (1-2 inches) and, like the bark, twigs and leaves are processed for their aromatic qualities (cinnamonaldehyde).

Traditional Use

From Eastern Asia the cassia had already reached the Hebrews in antiquity and was a component of their sacred incense mixtures. The incense effect is said to open the heart and induce relaxation and calmness. In small amounts it has a stimulating effect on the central nervous system. Asians also like to burn cassia because it repels insects.

Notes on Burning as Incense

The pleasant cinnamon/spicy and sweet/woody fragrance spreads agreeable warmth with a subtle peppery/sharp note in the background. It is very well suited to festive or sensual mixes.

Fragrance Message

Gentle guidance in the direction of sensitivity and opening for liberation from a state of paralysis.

'Stepping out of constriction'

CEDAR TIPS

Thuja plicata
Cypress, cupressaceae
Syn.: Flat cedar, cedar tips, Western red cedar
Part of plant: Twig tips
Elemental force: EARTH
Emphasis: EMOTION

Origin

This mighty conifer is especially at home on the West Coast of North America between California and Canada. It is valued for its high quality timber in ship building and for bridges. Actually it is not a genuine species of cedar but a giant *arbor vitae* that can live to 1,000 years of age and reach a height of 60 to 80 meters (180 to 240 feet).

Traditional Use

Native American tribes on the West Coast used the trunk of this tree to carve their famous totem poles. The aromatic tips of the spacious crown are a traditional Native American incense. According to the medicine man this is the feminine counterpart to white sage. The tips are burned in the bowl of an abalone shell and the strong aromatic smoke is said to unite the four elements of earth, water, air and fire.

Notes on Burning as Incense

The sweet dark/spicy fragrant smoke sensitizes us to the forces of the plant kingdom and makes a perfect offering to the plant spirits. It is similar to the frankincense cedar, and as a symbol of the connection between heaven and earth also harmonizes the bodymind during ritual work.

Fragrance Message

Drawing on the wisdom of the primordial being, we are guided towards our own inner strength with gentle steadfastness.

'Harmony grows out of a strong connection'

CEDAR WOOD

Juniperus virginiana
Cypress tree/Cypressaceae
Syn.: Red cedar, pencil cedar
Part of plant: Heartwood
Elemental force: EARTH
Emphasis: EMOTION

Origin

This species of cedar comes from North America and is actually classified as a juniper. It is similar to the European sade tree. An evergreen conifer native to the region east of the Rocky Mountains, it achieves a proud height of 35 meters (110 feet) with a trunk diameter of up to 1.5 meters (4.5 feet). A reddish heartwood exudes a strong aromatic fragrance. This tree displays a very dignified overall appearance.

Traditional Use

Cedar is an old Native American remedy for infections of the respiratory passages. It has a long history as a popular incense, said to unite the four elements with one another, creating a harmonious and sensuous mood and good fortune. According to tradition burning it promotes soul strength and groundedness. It is also a time-tested insect repellant.

Notes on Burning as Incense

The heartwood of the red cedar spreads an aromatic, warmly enveloping fragrance. Psychic/emotional aspects are of primary consideration on such an occasion. A protective and harmonizing element furthers an illumined peace of mind and restorative relaxation. Existence takes care.

Fragrance Message

Being guided back to the safety of the center where everything is right as it is and allowed to be as it is.

'Protection and power are here'

CINNAMON BARK

Cinnamomum cassia
Cinnamomum aromaticum nees
Bay plant/Lauraceae
Syn.: Chinese cinnamon
Part of plant: Bark
Elemental force: FIRE
Emphasis: BODY

Origin

This slender evergreen tree is a native of the subtropics of southern China. Pruned into a bush it is cultivated commercially and provides one of the oldest botanic commodities. It can also be found in Vietnam, Burma, Laos, Japan and India. Reaching a height of barely 3 meters (9 feet), the bark, twigs, buds and leaves are processed for their aromatic quality (cinnamonaldehyde).

Traditional Use

Traditional Chinese Medicine uses cinnamon as an internal warming remedy (yang), valuing its efficiency in treating colds, diarrhea, rheumatism, lumbago and impotence. It is said to strengthen the vital force (chi). Burning the bark may open the heart, imparting relaxation and inner peace. Small amounts have a stimulating effect on the central nervous system. More than 4,000 years ago cinnamon bark found its way to Egypt and Greece as an ingredient for religious incense. In occultism this incense is considered to be an aphrodisiac.

Notes on Burning as Incense

An important component of many incense mixtures, cinnamon bark can always be added to create a warm, cozy and opened hearted atmosphere. It immediately immerses a room in a homey yet stimulating, exotic mood. Good mixed with cardamom and bay leaves (Ayurvedic).

Fragrance Message

Familiar impulses trigger dreams and allow free flight of the imagination.

'Food for the inner fire'

CLOVE

Eugenia caryophyllata
Syzygium aromaticum
Myrtle plant/Myrtaceae
Part of plant: Buds
Elemental force: FIRE
Emphasis: BODY

Origin

This slender evergreen tree with a height of about 12 meters (40 feet) and smooth gray bark is said to originate in Indonesia. Today it is cultivated throughout the world especially in the Philippines, Moluccas and Madagascar. The dried flower buds of this tree are traded as cloves.

Traditional Use

Around the world clove buds are a familiar kitchen spice. As a medicinal tincture it is applied to skin infections and parasite infestations as well as toothache. Tea extract and clove oil are used in Traditional Chinese Medicine to ease nausea, bad breath and diarrhea. Clove buds are included in Indian, Tibetan and Japanese incense sticks.

The antiseptic effect of clove smoke was already recognized as valuable in the Middle Ages and was used to protect against forms of the plague. Clove smoke is said to be a very effective counter to all types of negative vibrations and attack, including those of aggressive insects. Burning the substance as incense is said to be sexually stimulating.

Notes on Burning as Incense

The typically intense, spicy clove fragrance mixes well with eaglewood, elemi, styrax, benzoin and frankincense. It can be easily modified with nutmeg and cinnamon to make up a tonifying mixture.

Fragrance Message

Recognizing the beginning and the end as two sides of the same coin and being able to let go of old burdens.

'Approaching something new with momentum'

COPAL

Protium copal
Bursera spp.
Balsamiferous plant/Burseraceae
Syn.: 'Brain of the Heavens'
Part of plant: Resin
Elemental force: AIR
Emphasis: MIND

Origin

The term copal encompasses the resins of many types of bursera including those of Asia and Africa. Its origin stems from the Aztec word *copalcoahuitl* and denotes the resin of a Central American balsam tree that grows to around 15 meters (45 feet) tall. Its light resin was called 'food of the gods' by the Mayans and considered sacred.

Traditional Use

In the early cultures of Central America copal was an incense used for initiations and divine vision. Cleansing and encouragement of clairvoyance are the beneficial qualities that make the bright copal so valuable for ritual ceremonies.

But they were also familiar with its medicinal properties, such as pain relief for toothache or infectious swelling, as well as its high degree of effectiveness for diarrhea. For the shamans of the rainforest certain types of protium were companions to ecstatic healing. In these societies copal is still traditionally used as a protective incense against magical attacks and witchcraft.

Notes on Burning as Incense

The fragrance is distinguished by a bright and clear somewhat lemony/aromatic grace and can be easily burned alone either on a sieve or on coals. It purifies the inner attitude and supports mental/spiritual work.

Fragrance Message

Opening the heart and clearing the mind, inner peace and freshness join together for healing.

'Opening to the light'

CORIANDER

Coriandrum sativum
Umbellate plant/Apiaceae
Syn.: Chinese parsley
Part of plant: Fruit
Elemental force: WATER
Emphasis: EMOTION

Origin

This aromatic annual meadow plant is a native of Europe and Western Asia but has also spread to North America. It grows up to 1 meter (3 feet), has finely pinnate light green leaves and pink colored umbels in which the round brown fruits mature.

Traditional Use

Coriander capsules have been found in the tombs of the ancient Egyptians who burned them as incense. The seed is used as a kitchen spice and as a medicinal remedy primarily for digestive disorders. In Chinese naturopathy it is used to treat dysentery, hemorrhoids, measles, toothache, colds and ill health. Coriander is also helpful for migraine and neuralgic complaints, nervous exhaustion and general weakness. The Romans included coriander seeds in their love potions and the Arabs use it as a love incense.

Notes on Burning as Incense

This is an attunement remedy (Ayurveda) with a narcotic effect. The smoke can help alleviate nervous strain. An aphrodisiac mood develops after the slightly burnt smelling first impression gives way to a fine spicy aroma. It has a harmonizing effect. Can be combined well with benzoin, frankincense, myrrh and mastic.

Fragrance Message

All obstructive and destructive forces are pacified. This leads to harmony and a willingness to make contact.

'Creating equilibrium and calm'

COSTUS ROOT

Saussurea lappa
Saussurea costus
Aplotaxis costus
Aplotaxis auriculata
Composite/Asteraceae
Part of plant: Root
Elemental force: EARTH
Emphasis: EMOTION

Origin

This large perennial plant with its thick tap root grows upright to a height of 2 meters (6 feet), and on the tip develops many flowers that are almost black. Its home is northern India and it is closely related to the inula (Inula helenium), which is at home in Europe.

Traditional Use

As an ancient Ayurvedic remedy the root is used for disorders of the digestive system (including infections such as cholera and typhus) and respiratory complaints (as incense to treat asthma). It too is an ancient incense shown to be effective in the case of nervous tension, states of weakness and stress. The Arabs use the costus root in sensual incense mixtures. Perfumery also values the aphrodisiac, narcotic fragrance of this root.

In addition it can be used as a repellant against vermin.

Notes on Burning as Incense

This is an intense, earthy/sweet fragrance well suited to help us instinctively find our own center in moments when we lack orientation. With its erotic to animalistic stimulus it is also good to use in sensuous incense mixtures.

Fragrance Message

A powerful push into the positive realm where life shows its bright colors.

DAMIANA

Turnera diffusa willd
Turnera Aphrodisiaca
Saffron-mallow plant/Turneraceae
Syn.: *hierba del pastor*
'asthma-broom,' 'shirt-remover'
Part of plant: Herbage
Elemental force: FIRE
Emphasis: EMOTION

Origin

This flowering foliage plant is found in forested regions from Southern California to Argentina. It is most frequently encountered in Mexico where it is also extensively cultivated.

Traditional Use

In Native American medicine the leaves are burned as a remedy for asthma among other things. The plant is known as an aphrodisiac in Mexico while in the Caribbean it is an indispensable component in the cocktail of a love potion designed to spark passion in the desired man. It is also smoked together with hemp. The slightly euphoric character of the herb is highly valued. Tonifying, stimulating and relaxing, it brightens the mood.

Notes on Burning as Incense

The incense fragrance of damiana is green/herbal hot and tends to die down directly on the sieve. It is very good in a combination with copal and cassia, always adding its very own aromatic sweetish/green tone to the mix. It is well suited as a love incense.

Fragrance Message

A powerful impulse that aims at opening and devotion, imparting a sense of lightness and awakening the joy of life.

'Following the call of sensuality'

91

DAMMAR

Canarium strictum
Shorea wiesneri
Dipterous fruit plant/
Dipterocarpaceae
Syn.: Damar
Part of plant: Resin
Elemental force: AIR
Emphasis: MIND

Origin

This white resin comes from a tree that is a native of south-east Asia and occurs there with relative frequency. However it is important to know that a variety of resins of darker color are sometimes also traded under the name of dammar. The genuine resin is light to transparent and dusty white.

Traditional Use

In its place of origin dammar has traditionally been used as an incense for protection and cleansing. Since it is increasingly used in the industrial production of lacquers, varnishes and adhesives dammar is exported in large quantities across the world. Perfumery also uses it as a fixing agent.

In the Malaysian language the word dammar means 'light' and the resin itself also has refractive properties. When a dark mood prevails burning this resin as incense can affect a shift.

It connects us with transcendental realms and brings inspiration.

Notes on Burning as Incense

Burning dammar as an incense leads intensely into the mental realm and very clearly activates the mind. It is also quite suitable for occasions in which spiritual work is to be done. The bright fresh/fine to citrus fragrance works like a ray of light. It clarifies diffuse mental states and is also said to bear the gift of clairvoyance.

Fragrance Message

The fine vibrations of ethereal forces gather and connect with the seeker.

'Brightness flows through you'

DRAGON BLOOD

Daemenorops draco
Calamus draco willd.
Palm plant/Arecaceae
Syn.: Sumatra dragon's blood,
Sang-Dragon
Part of plant: Resin
Elemental force: FIRE
Emphasis: BODY

Origin

The dracaena palm, a tree whose shape is reminiscent of a primeval world can be found in the swampy regions of Asia, Africa and Australia. The flower and fruit exude a red resin that is available on the market. The Canarese dragon tree *(Dracena cinnabari)* is an attraction of the Canary Islands and also supplies a red dragon blood resin but this is not commercially relevant.

Traditional Use

This incense substance is steeped in legend and is often associated with mythological stories. It appears to radiate invincibility and martial powers and has always had magical forces attributed to it. With its medicinal/cosmetic effect, Pliny already mentions it as a component of an ancient rose ointment.

Dragon Blood does however deserve particular mention because of its relevance as an ingredient in ritual incense for protection and offerings. Its quality as a fixing and boosting agent for cleansing mixtures is indispensable in the production of frankincense for the Church.

Notes on Burning as Incense

The dark/tart somewhat gum-like burnt smelling fragrance develops a penetrating power in a cleansing incense combined with frankincense. A very sensual mix can be achieved along with sandalwood, cedar and labdanum.

Fragrance Message

Indecisiveness and timidity are transformed with an intense burst of fire into

'Strength and courage'

EAGLEWOOD

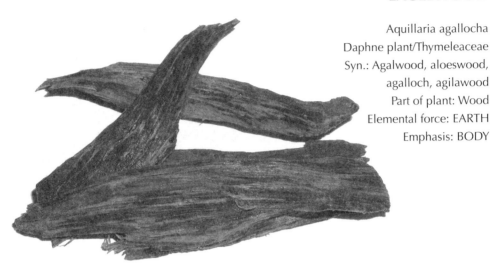

Aquillaria agallocha
Daphne plant/Thymeleaceae
Syn.: Agalwood, aloeswood,
agalloch, agilawood
Part of plant: Wood
Elemental force: EARTH
Emphasis: BODY

Origin

The eaglewood tree can be found deep in the forests of Assam, as well as in Indonesia, Cambodia, and Vietnam. The noble fragrance of this wood is only produced during the decaying process when it is invaded by a certain type of fungus (phomopsis aquillariae). In the throes of death the tree develops a defensive balm against this parasitic invasion. This allows parts of the wood to become waterproof, resistant to decay and often heavier than water.

Traditional Uses

The value of this wood depends upon its resinous, dark and heavy qualities which is why it is even weighed in gold when it changes hands. It is a component of the most expensive Japanese incense (Jinkoh) and is also held in high esteem in the Arabian world. The Sufis claim that the oil (Ud) has a strong transformational force as it provides support in the transition between life and death. Ayurvedic and Tibetan medicines use it to relieve illnesses of the mind and sadness of the heart. In Traditional Chinese Medicine eaglewood is said to strongly activate the *chi* (vital force).

Notes on Burning as Incense

Incense with eaglewood can induce a state of trance and contemplation while at the same time greatly increasing awareness. Use with much respect!

Fragrance Message

A delightful scent, deeply profound and dignified aromatic form of expressing a gesture of humility before the

Wonder of Creation.
'Completion and coming home'

ELEMI RESINOID

Canarium luzonicum
Canarium commune
Balsamiferous plant/Burseraceae
Syn.: Manila elemi
Part of plant: Herbage
Elemental force: FIRE
Emphasis: MIND

Origin

This tropical tree, which grows up to 30 meters (90 feet), is native to the Philippines and the Moluccas (Spice Islands) and is also cultivated there. When the bark is punctured it exudes a sap of resin and essential oils that has a very acrid smell. After a long period of drying it solidifies into a soft paste and is then turned into a more solid resinoid through an extraction process.

Traditional Use

As an oleoresin, elemi is used in its native lands for skincare, respiratory diseases and as a general stimulant. The ancient Egyptians are said to have used it for embalming. Elemi is mentioned as an ingredient in many old incense recipes for cleansing and clearing. The refreshing properties of this resin activate and purify the human energy centers.

Notes on Burning as Incense

When we are exhausted or when mental activity is called for this fresh/green clearing fragrance can deliver a powerful burst of energy. It's a good morning incense. For grounding some sandalwood can be added to counter the danger of spacing out. Be careful when burning this incense on the sieve, Elemi is extremely flammable!

Fragrance Message

A positive, hopeful hint from life suggesting you use the many possibilities it offers.

'Setting off for new horizons'

EUCALYPTUS

Eucalyptus dives
Myrtle plant/Myrtaceae
Syn.: Gum tree
Part of plant: Fruit
Elemental force: FIRE
Emphasis: BODY

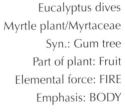

Origin

This robust medium sized eucalyptus tree has a short trunk, broad branches and fibrous gray bark. It grows in Australia and Tasmania. In the early stages its leaves are heart shaped and blue-green, tapering to a point at both ends. Its fruit forms small clusters arranged in a star shape on slender stalks along the stem. Leaves, twigs and fruit all have strong fragrance.

Traditional Use

The Aborigines say that "heat leaves the sick person and goes into the fire" when the leaves and twigs of the gum tree are burned. They use this medicine to bring down fevers. The cleansing, pressure and pain relieving effects of essential eucalyptus oil ease infections of the respiratory passages, strengthen the immune and the nervous systems, and can also be of benefit when this substance is burned as an incense. It can clear thoughts and help fight off destructive influences.

Notes on Burning as Incense

The powerful medicinal fragrance of this incense is used to achieve an activating and energizing effect. It helps improve respiration and goes well with physical exercise.

Fragrance Message

A hot/cold contrast has a polarizing effect on our existence. The inner swamps are drained and concentration is coolly directed toward survival.

'Stepping from swathes of fog into clarity'

FENNEL SEED

Foeniculum vulgare
Anethum foeniculum
Umbellate plant/Apiaceae
Syn.: Fennel
Part of plant: Seed
Elemental force: WATER
Emphasis: EMOTION

Origin

Fennel is a biennial or perennial that grows up to 1.8 meters (6 feet). It has a large root, filigree pinnate leaves and golden yellow flowers arranged in umbels from which large clusters form in turn. The wild form thrives in Southern Europe and it is also widespread as a cultivated garden plant throughout Europe.

Traditional Use

Fennel is an ancient remedy thought to promote longevity, courage and strength. It is also used for its neutralizing and antispasmodic effect on digestive disorders (liver, spleen, gallbladder), as well as both detoxifying and strengthening the eye. The estrogen-like effect which also promotes milk formation in nursing mothers, indicates its relationship to all things feminine. According to tradition burning fennel as incense helps keep away evil spirits.

Notes on Burning as Incense

The anise related fragrance with its slightly woodsy tone mixes well with lavender and sandalwood. As it is somewhat more pungent than anise it is advisable to use it in mixtures rather than alone. Crush the seed capsules in advance with a mortar and pestle since they may otherwise burst on the fire with a small bang. It alleviates feelings of loneliness.

Fragrance Message

The impulse toward a solution and the clearing of accumulated problems leads us home into a sense of security and inner stability.

'Comfort and relaxation'

FRANKINCENSE

Boswellia carteri
Boswellia sacra
Balsamiferous tree/Burseraceae
Syn.: Olibanum
Part of plant: Resin
Elemental force: FIRE
Emphasis: BODY

Origin

The resin of the frankincense tree, whose history is so closely tied to the esthetic and spiritual development of humanity, comes from north-eastern Africa and the countries around the Red Sea. This relatively small tree is distinguished by its low spiral shape. It grows at the edge of the desert on barren sun parched land with minimal moisture. The wound resin that it exudes in teardrops acts as protection from the sun.

Traditional Use

Olibanum is one of our most important incense. In addition to the species listed above there is also the Indian frankincense (*Boswellia serrata*) that has similar properties. From the medicinal perspective frankincense is recommended for skin care, to treat respiratory diseases, urogenital disorders, nervous stress and according to the latest findings for rheumatic complaints. It has exceptional significance for cleansing, meditation and sensitization to higher vibrations and is used throughout the world in the production of incense.

Notes on Burning as Incense

Frankincense is very helpful alone or in mixtures as a cleansing incense and for the reduction of nervous tensions. A bright fragrance with a slight citrus note is proof of quality.

Fragrance Message

The laws of life become clear when physical existence is endowed with spirituality.

'Letting the truth in'

FUMARIA

Fumaria officinalis
Poppy plant/Papaveraceae
Syn.: Fumitory, fume weed, earth-smoke
Part of plant: Herbage
Elemental force: FIRE
Emphasis: BODY

Origin

This annual plant grows throughout Europe on barren wastelands, in ruins and along roadsides. It reaches a height of 30 to 70 cm (12 to 28 inches) and has either a creeping or upright stem with many branches, forms pinnate leaves and produces pink to purple clusters of blossoms.

Traditional Use

As a strong cleansing medicinal herb fumaria is valued for its purgative and bile stimulating effects as well as its protective effect on vision. Contrasting effects on circulation and respiration are attributed to it at higher dosages (= numbing) and lower dosages (= stimulating). It is thought to be an ancient Celtic incense and was used in the Middle Ages for exorcizing demons and establishing contact with the intermediate world. As such it also plays a significant role in witchcraft. For the occultists it stands under the influence of Mars and Saturn, which they see as the reason for its drying and cleansing properties.

Notes on Burning as Incense

This herb has an intensely polarizing effect but not a very attractive fragrance! As incense it is best to burn together with frankincense and camphor. It helps resolve indecision.

Fragrance Message

An influence that brings the process *to the razor's edge*. Leading to action and raising the question:

'Reality or illusion?'

GALANGAL

Alpinia galanga
Ginger plant/Zingiberaceae
Syn.: Galingale, calangall, greater galagal
Part of plant: Root
Elemental force: FIRE
Emphasis: BODY

Origin

This reed-like plant grows wild in forested areas on the southern side of the Himalayas. It also grows in Thailand and China. The stems achieve a height of up to 2 meters (6 feet) and the powerful root system (rhizome) can extend for a meter (3 feet). Well known as a very old remedy, the ancient Egyptians, Greeks and Romans already traded galangal root from south-eastern Asia.

Traditional Use

According to St. Hildegard of Bingen (*Holistic Healing*, 800 years ago) galangal helps in disabilities related to mobility and problems of the heart caused by a dishonest emotional life. Ayurveda uses it for disorders of the respiratory passages as well as for rheumatic complaints. It has a stimulating and digestive effect which also makes it a preferred spice in the Indonesian kitchen.

Notes on Burning as Incense

Hot and peppery with a slight camphor tone these hard pieces of root unfold their energizing strength over an extended period of time. Ginger is well suited for activating and stimulating incense mixtures which include dammar (air) and lavender (water).

Fragrance Message

It is time to release whatever keeps you in a state of constriction and suffering. This is an aromatic impulse to give you trust in your own strength. It can lead you into the process of healing.

'Aiming at the goal and being open to it'

GALBANUM RESINOID

Ferula galbaniflua
Ferula gummosa
Umbellate plant/Apiaceae
Syn.: Galbanum
Part of plant: Root
Elemental force: EARTH
Emphasis: EMOTION

Origin

This tall perennial fennel like umbel plant grows from 1 to 2 meters (3 to 6 feet) in height in its native habitat in the Near East and western Asia. Cuts are made at its base just above the root to tap the milk-like oleoresin which solidifies into a brown sticky paste when dried. Mostly what is available on the market is the harder Iranian galbanum. There is also a softer quality from Afghanistan (Leviathan).

Traditional Use

Since ancient times galbanum has been used as an important incense and healing remedy. It has proved to be medicinally effective for skin care, neuralgia, muscle pain, nervous strain, digestive disorders and respiratory diseases. Known as a pain relieving antidote and remedy to aid the expulsion of miscarriages, it is burned as an incense for epilepsy and gynecological problems.

Notes on Burning as Incense

Cleansing incense with this woodsy green fragrant smoke is a good medium for driving away spirits that we have called upon. It helps resolve unclear feelings, alien energies and the resulting imaginary conflicts. Added to incense combinations it strengthens authenticity.

Fragrance Message

The awakening of consciousness creates a contact with the essence and masks can fall.

'Calmness and grounding develop'

GINGER LILY

Kaempferia galanga
Ginger plant/Zingiberaceae
Part of plant: Root
Elemental force: FIRE
Emphasis: EMOTION

Origin

This ginger plant comes from India where it grows abundantly in gardens everywhere. Its root tuber supplies an important Ayurvedic remedy by the name of *Kapoor Kachali* or sometimes *Kachiri*. While a remedy from a similar plant of the genus *Hedychium spicatum* is made in Northern India and has 'north' included in its name, *Kaempferia galanga* grows in southern India and is tagged the 'south walla' to distinguish it.

Traditional Use

Kapoor Kachali is applied to the scalp to improve hair growth. It is also used for coughs and problems of the respiratory passages, and as a skin powder during *Holi* Festival celebrations. From ancient times the tuber of the ginger lily has been added to stimulating *dhoops,* a cone-shaped form of incense, as well as to incense mixtures in general. It is also known as a nerve tonic and treatment for depression.

Notes on Burning as Incense

A fiery/spicy ginger-like fragrance makes this aromatic root a special experience with its highly stimulating properties. It is also particularly well suited to special incense mixtures. Relatively easy to crush into a fine powder, it readily absorbs aroma oils and resinoids.

Fragrance Message

Activity and zest are created. Pleasure and vitality are equally necessary to celebrate existence.

'Take advantage of the moment of lightness'

GINGER

Zingiber officinale
Ginger plant/Zingiberaceae
Part of plant: Root tuber
Elemental force: FIRE
Emphasis: BODY

Origin

Ginger originated in south-east Asia and is now cultivated everywhere in the tropics. It is grown from Africa to the Caribbean, China to Japan. This is a perennial plant that reaches a height of up to 1 meter (3 feet) and develops a thick, prolific root system from which emerges a reed-like stem with narrow lance shaped leaves giving white or yellow flowers.

Traditional Use

In the East ginger root has been used for centuries as a kitchen spice and home remedy for many types of complaint, such as rheumatism, dysentery, toothaches, diarrhea and malaria. Its effectiveness is especially valued for digestive disorders but it is also used as a fragrance in cosmetics and perfumes as well as a flavoring in food and drinks. In Zen Buddhism ginger is one of the seven important incense substances.

Notes on Burning as Incense

The typically sweet, hot fragrance of ginger-root burned as incense has a very warming and mobilizing effect on our initiative and ability to make decisions. It mixes especially well with eaglewood, sandalwood, cinnamon, cloves and camphor.

Fragrance Message

A powerful aromatic burst of fire that leads us out of rigidity and lets the energy flow freely to overcome blocks.

'Life is movement'

GRAY SAGE

Artemisia tridentata, californica, ludoviciana
frigida, douglasiana
Composite/Asteraceae
Syn.: Desert Sage, Gray Sage, Sage Brush
Part of Plant: Herbage
Elemental force: EARTH
Emphasis: BODY

Origin

This bushy aromatic wormwood covers wide parts of the high desert country in Western USA and is especially native to Nevada. There are five to six different species with male and female types. It grows to a height of 1.30 to 1.60 meters (4 to 5 feet), has small gray elongated leaves and gives off an intense fragrance especially after rain.

Traditional Use

'Sage brush' is perhaps the oldest and most highly respected incense in the Native American culture. Sometimes it is also called 'salvia' even though it belongs to the artemisia and not the salvia family. In addition to its great medicinal value for coughs, colds, headaches, painful swellings and constipation, it possesses sudorific and febrifugal qualities. Native Americans consider it a strong repellant against vermin, parasitic fungal growth and all types of bacteria.

The greatest significance of sage brush is however in ritual use during spiritual ceremonies. Burning it as incense connects Mother Earth with the Great Spirit. Powerfully does it drive away bad feelings and negative thoughts.

Notes on Burning as Incense

The intensely herbal smoke activates inner strength. It is good for use against weakness and discouragement.

Fragrance Message

A mighty protective shield against every type of misfortune is created.

'Preservation of life'

GUAIACUM WOOD

Guaiacum officinale
Guaiacum coulteri, palmeri, sanctum
Yoke-leaf plant/Zygophyllaceae
Syn.: Brazil wood, lignun vitae
Part of plant: Wood
Elemental force: EARTH
Emphasis: EMOTION

Origin

This evergreen tropical tree attains a height of from 10 to 13 meters (30 to 39 feet). It has extremely hard wood (heavier than water) and is a native of the mountains and forests of Central America and the Caribbean. When exposed to the sun the bark naturally exudes an aromatic resin which is as significant for naturopathic healing as the wood itself. Originally yellow, the wood oxidizes in air and turns bluish gray. When burned as incense its color changes again to a reddish hue as it exudes the dark resinoid in a clearly visible manner.

Traditional Use

The natives of the Americas—even as early as the Aztecs—used the aromatic products of this tree, also called *palo santo* (holy wood), for both medicine and ritual. It was burned as incense for coughs and colds. In the 16th Century it came to Europe as a remedy for syphilis (lues). Because of its hardness Native Americans use this wood as a sympathetic stimulus for impaired male potency. Because of its particularly euphoric effect it is suitable as a sensitizing aphrodisiac.

Notes on Burning as Incense

The vanilla-like soft fragrance has a subduing and soothing effect on a passionate temperament but a stimulating one when there is fearful restraint.

Fragrance Message

This is the story of the hard shell that covers the soft kernel.

'Sensitivity and strength are united here'

GUGGUL

Commiphora mukul
Balsamodendron agollocha
Balsamiferous plant/Burseraceae
Syn.: Indian bdellium, guggula
Part of plant: Resin
Elemental force: WATER
Emphasis: EMOTION

Origin

This small thorny shrub-like tree is native to dry stony areas in central and northern India and Pakistan. The resin is harvested by scoring the bark of trees growing in the wild. Its survival is now endangered because of years of destructive exploitation.

Traditional Use

Guggul is among the most important natural remedies of India and the Ayurvedic approach to health. It is greatly valued for its regulative effect on the digestive system and female genital organs. It has a stimulating effect on the internal secretions and is detoxifying and a strong disinfectant. Guggul has a healing effect on the skin and is a treatment for nervous disorders. Furthermore it is known to be a good aphrodisiac. Since ancient times it has been available in Europe under the name of *Indian bdellium*. It plays an important role in India,

Nepal and Tibet because of its psychoactive medicinal, magical and spiritual qualities.

Notes on Burning as Incense

The incense fragrance is very intense ranging from sweet/balsamic to vanilla-like with tart/resinous tones. Guggul can help free the nervous system of many toxins. When burned as incense it relieves tensions and engenders a state of deep peace and serenity. Effective for repelling mosquitoes too.

Fragrance Message

All disruptive influences must be released and only what has vital significance remains.

'Feeling into the depths'

GUM ARABIC

Acacia senegal willd.
Acacia spp.
Mimose plant/Mimosaceae
Syn.: Kordofan gum
Part of plant: Resin
Elemental force: AIR
Emphasis: EMOTION

Origin

A gum resin can be extracted from more than one hundred different species of acacia. Of these, Australian and American acacia species contain a psychoactive alkaloid while some of the African resins are even poisonous. What is known as gum Arabic comes from about ten different African/Indian species. These are bushy trees whose bark gives up a gum-like sap that dries into glassy water soluble chips.

Traditional Use

The acacias that supply this resin were already popular in the Middle Ages. Its use in folk medicine has a long history because it relieves fever, tumors, eye disease, diarrhea and gynecological disorders. Today the resin plays an important role as a binding agent in the paint and food industries.

It has also been used since ancient times as a binding agent for incense mixtures because it has almost no smell of its own when burned. The gum is considered a tonic and an aphrodisiac, making a person aware of and sensitive to the world around him.

Notes on Burning as Incense

As a powdered material it is an ideal carrier for essential oils to be added to incense mixtures. When it is moistened it makes a paste that can be kneaded with various materials and hardens when it dries.

Fragrance Message

Devotedly surrendering to what is striving to manifest, wanting to be perceived.

'Development of form through transparency'

HIMALAYAN JUNIPER

Juniperus macropoda
Juniperus semiglobosa
Cypress plant/Cypressaceae
Syn.: Tibetan *shug pa*
Part of plant: Twig tips
Elemental force: FIRE
Emphasis: MIND

Origin

This is a powerful plant that bushes or grows as a tree up to 10 or 20 meters (30 to 60 feet) in height. In the Himalayas it can be found at elevations up to 4000 meters (12,000 feet). The higher the elevation the more this tree is considered sacred and in possession of powerful spirits. The nature of these elevations causes very intense aromatic characteristics to develop.

Traditional Use

The people of the Himalayas burn incense made from the twig tips of this juniper species as part of daily cleansing and protection rituals in their houses. It is an important component of the Tibetan incense culture.

This juniper has a disinfectant and intensely room cleansing effect, even purging very unpleasant smells. It is also used as an insect and mosquito repellant.

Defense against negative influences is effective on all levels. The smoke is called 'food of the gods' and has special significance in shamanic exorcism rituals and for trance states.

Notes on Burning as Incense

When burned as incense the twig tips give off a fragrance that ranges from aromatic spicy/resinous to woody. This incense is recommended for the refinement of sensory perception when seeking a vision.

Fragrance Message

A strong hand leads you into the realm of the transcendent to an experience of unity.

'Inner connection with the whole'

HIMALAYAN SAGE

Artemisia tibet.
A. caruifolia, A. dubia,
A. roxburghiana
Composite/Asteraceae
Syn.: Ganden Khaenpa, titepati,
nagdhen, nagdhamani
Part of plant: Herbage
Elemental force: AIR
Emphasis: MIND

Origin

This strong upright wormwood grows throughout the Himalayas at between 1500 and 3600 meters (4,500 and 10,800 feet). It is particularly harvested around the Ganden Monastery near Lhasa. Intense radiation of the sun at these altitudes causes an especially high concentration of essential oil and a correspondingly potent fragrance.

Traditional Use

Great medicinal value has been attributed to this plant. It is used in Ayurveda as an antispasmodic and tonifying remedy for nervous and spastic complaints especially asthma and headaches. It has traditionally been burned as an offering to Shiva and also at funerals. At Tibetan New Year celebrations this mugwort also serves as a ritual agent supporting this transition. Again and again it opens the threshold to new dimensions where the cleansing strength of artemisia is sought after in order to ensure a successful transformation.

Notes on Burning as Incense

Together with juniper this herb is outstandingly well suited as a cleansing incense. It is also highly recommended for incense rituals which strive for protection and defense against negative energies. It opens the way when we want to head for new horizons.

Fragrance Message

Inner peace and clarity are created and attention is powerfully directed toward the new tasks.

'Opening up and risking the step'

INDIAN SARSAPARILLA

Hemidesmus indicus
Swallowwort plant/Asclepiadaceae
Syn.: Sugandhi
Part of plant: Root
Elemental Force: EARTH
Emphasis: EMOTION

Origin

This milky herb can be found on the plains of the upper Ganges toward the east all the way to Bengal, and from Madhya Pradesh to southern India. It is a perennial, creeping, vine-like plant with a woody fragrant root system. The slender stalk has adversifoliate lance shaped narrow leaves with greenish flowers in the rachis.

Traditional Use

It is mentioned in the literature of ancient India as an important medicine. Especially for skin problems it is known for its anti-inflammatory, nourishing, and protective effect and is also used to relieve a poor appetite and gastrointestinal disorders. Moreover it is a febrifuge with a cooling, tonifying and cleansing effect on the entire organism. Hemidesmus indicus is stimulating for the flow of all fluids. A watery extract of the root is used to promote hair growth and using this plant as incense is said to promote health and vitality.

Notes on Burning as Incense

The fragrance of this root stems from the portion of cumarin which creates a vanilla-like soft atmosphere and is extremely stimulating because of its provocative sweetness.

Fragrance Message

A delicate but clearly tangible impulse that manifests itself in a restorative and motivating manner in the physical and emotional bodies.

'In good hands and supported'

INULA

Inula helenium
Composite/Asteraceae
Syn.: Elecampane, horseheal,
horseheel.
Part of plant: Root
Elemental force: WATER
Emphasis: MIND

Origin

This powerful plant grows as a bush of up to 3 meters (10 feet) in height, preferring banks and moist forests. It is however also very drought tolerant. Today it is common in North America although it probably originally came from Europe and Asia. Having a robust, hairy stem and oval leaves that taper to a point and are velvety soft on the underside, it has large golden yellow composite flowers and a large fleshy root.

Traditional Use

Inula is an ancient medicinal herb with a vast number of traditional names and applications that range from medicinal to magical and religious. The Slavs especially consider it to be a defensive and magical remedy. It has proved its healing power on the 'black death' for the Wends. The Latin name *Inula* means *emptying* and *cleansing*. It was associated with Odin's runes—*wind* and *breath*.

An expectorant, it releases obstructive waste materials and is supportive of general well being. The power of the sun works through this substance and its fragrance is said to drive out the modern demons of stress and depression. People in the Austrian province of Styria still burn incense with inula on Christmas Eve, for in Christian symbolism it represents redemption through the light of Christ.

Notes on Burning as Incense

A very pleasant fragrance like banana and freshly baked bread that creates a protective, bright atmosphere.

Fragrance Message

With every breath more clarity and calmness is created on my path with its goal of essential knowledge about everything.

'Light from the root'

JUNIPER BERRIES

Juniperus communis
Cypress tree/Cupressaceae
Syn.: Common juniper, malmot berries
Part of plant: Berries
Elemental force: FIRE
Emphasis: MIND

Origin

This small evergreen tree is at home in the northern hemisphere of our planet. A conifer which can be found from northern Asia to the Baltic, from northern Europe to Canada, it grows up to about 6 meters (18 feet) and develops small berries that are green in the first year only to turn blue-black during the second and third year.

Traditional Use

Juniper is useful for urinary and gastrointestinal infections, worms, disorders of the respiratory passages, gout, rheumatism and arthritis. It is also said to heal wounds and be effective against all types of parasites. Since ancient times the twigs and berries have been burned during incense rituals. They have been an indispensable part of shamanic cultures and are considered capable of providing magical protection. In Germany too it is counted among the most important of magical plants.

Notes on Burning as Incense

A wonderful aromatic fragrance spreads when these berries are burned. Crushed, they can be used very well in mixtures together with, for example, vetiver, mastic, elemi, galbanum, cedar and oakmoss. They are also suitable as a general repellant.

Fragrance Message

Strengthening the power of the self so that with clarity of vision things can be seen as they are.

'Inner peace and trust'

JUNIPER TIPS

Juniperus scopulorum
Cypress tree/Cupressaceae
Syn.: Rocky Mountain Juniper
Part of plant: Twig tips
Elemental force: FIRE
Emphasis: MIND

Origin

As the traditional name implies this juniper grows in the Rocky Mountains. It is a bushy tree rarely reaching more than 3 meters (9 feet) and forms small greenish blue berries.

Traditional Use

The juniper holds a special ritual position in all of the incense cultures of the world. The Rocky Mountain juniper has always been valued highly among the Native American tribes of this region as a power plant that is 'detoxifying' in both the physical and emotional sense. They believe that it purifies negative states and simultaneously strengthens the body's defenses. It is also burned in sweatlodge ceremonies, for the Sun Dance or to purify a place, the body and the ritual implements. Furthermore, it is used to clear the body and mind to become open for visionary experiences.

Notes on Burning as Incense

The powerful fragrance of this aromatic plant is so special and all encompassing in its effectiveness that it is quite appropriate to burn it alone, while completely opening to this experience.

Fragrance Message

Out of its smoke a great green power unfurls into the moment. Encounter it with respect.

'A presence that offers confidence'

113

LABDANUM

Cistus ladaniferus
Cistus creticus
Rockrose plant/Cistaceae
Syn.: Ladanum
Part of plant: Resin
Elemental force: WATER
Emphasis: EMOTION

Origin

This small bush with beautiful flowers similar to the dog rose reaches a height of 1 to 3 meters (3 to 9 feet). It is native to the mountainous regions of the Mediterranean, especially Greece, Cypress and Morocco but is also found in Portugal, Spain, Southern France and in the Balkans. Rockrose gum is an oleoresin exuded by this plant and is gathered by boiling plant matter in water. In earlier times goats were driven through the rockrose macchia and the sticky resin was then combed from their coats.

Traditional Use

Ladanum was keenly sought after in ancient times for its medicinal value is extensive. Applications include use in personal grooming (for wrinkles and hair loss), as a stimulant for menstruation, and its qualities as a fixing agent and fragrance in perfumes made it a favorite scent of the Minoan women. It was consecrated to Aphrodite the Goddess of Love. Together with calamus root and styrax, ladanum was mixed into *chypre* and has always been an extremely important ingredient in incense.

Notes on Burning as Incense

The complex fragrance, which is reminiscent of musk/ambergris, carries people away on imaginary journeys into worlds of the senses and the body. Mixtures including ladanum can be easily turned into little balls of incense. A beautiful combination comes from blending it with juniper, cedar and mastic.

Fragrance Message

At the still point of focused awareness we can draw from the abundance of life.

'Discover the wonder of the senses'

LAVENDER

Lavandula angustifolia
Lavandula vera
Labiate/Lamiaceae
Syn.: Spike, aspic
Part of plant: Flowers
Elemental force: WATER
Emphasis: MIND

Origin

This is an evergreen, strongly fragrant herbaceous plant with a woody base that grows up to 1 meter (3 feet). It has light green narrow leaves and violet-blue flower panicles on long naked stems. It originally came from the Mediterranean area and is now cultivated throughout the entire world.

Traditional Use

Almost everyone is familiar with the fragrance of lavender. It is one of the most time tested folk remedies in the world. The essential oil is used to provide a fragrance that is both an invigorating as well as soothing, calming remedy. It is regarded as the most versatile of essences.

It provides effective help for all types of problems whether for the locomotive system, circulation, respiratory passages, digestive and immune systems, urogenital tract or the nervous system. Last but not least it works well as an insect repellant.

As an incense lavender finds its origins in the Minoan tradition and it is still used in church frankincense mixtures today.

Notes on Burning as Incense

Lavender has a fresh/sweet to delicate/camphor fragrance impression that is suitable for cleansing and clearing. It combines very well in relaxing mixtures together with cedar wood, mastic, pine resin, oakmoss and many other substances but is also fine to burn alone as incense.

Fragrance Message

This peaceful impulse gently leads us in the direction of clearing and creates connection.

'Shedding light on the emotions'

LEMON GRASS

Cymbopogon citratus
Andropogon citratus
Sweet grasses/Poaceae
Part of plant: Leaves, blades
Elemental force: FIRE
Emphasis: MIND

Origin

Originally from Asia this fast growing aromatic grass is mainly cultivated in India but is also grown in the Caribbean and Africa. In tropical regions it can grow to a height of 1.5 meters (4.5 feet) and develops an extensive root system that can quickly exhaust the soil.

Traditional Use

Traditional medicine in India is familiar with its healing effect on feverish infections and its calming influence on the central nervous system. This has been confirmed by modern research. Furthermore, its essential oil is renowned as an anti-depressive, nerve strengthening and pain relieving remedy. As a fragrance it is often used in soaps, cosmetics and perfumes as well as in food and drinks. It is also listed as one of the incense components in kyphi recipes.

Notes on Burning as Incense

For morning meditations and situations where fresh momentum is necessary this grass, with its opening and stimulating qualities is a good addition to an incense mix. A lemony inspiring fragrance develops quickly and creates activating energy.

Fragrance Message

An optimistic mood arises. There is a sunny freshness that imparts joy and inspiration.

'Welcome the new'

LOBAN

Styrax benzoin
Styrax plant/Styraceae
Syn.: Lobhan, luban
Calcutta block benzoin
Part of plant: Resin/gum mix
Elemental force: WATER
Emphasis: EMOTION

Origin

Loban is the generic Hindu name for frankincense resins. Guggul (Commiphora mukul) and Indian frankincense (Boswellia serrata) are sometimes also sold under this name. Usually however what we are dealing with is the so-called Calcutta block benzoin. Although also known as

Sumatra benzoin it is actually a mixture together with other gums and resins, for which there are countless secret recipes in Malaysia and Indonesia. The resulting concoctions are then pressed into blocks of correspondingly different qualities and sold via Calcutta and north-eastern India.

Traditional Use

The high proportion of pure Sumatra benzoin allows this special incense preparation to be used in contexts similar to those of benzoin. However loban is more commonly found in the folk usage of incense especially on the In-

dian subcontinent. Loban is also an important constituent of *dhoop* sticks which are used both medicinally and as religious smoke offerings.

Notes on Burning as Incense

The sometimes heavy sweetness of the block benzoin can produce a hypnotic sultry mood with a sensual quality. It has a seductive, harmonizing and mood enhancing effect.

Fragrance Message

An enveloping, soothing protective cloak inviting us to relax and dream.

'Allow yourself to let go and surrender'

117

LUPULIN (HOPS)

Humulus lupulus
Mulberry plant/Cannabaceae
Syn.: Hops
Part of plant: Pollen
Elemental force: WATER
Emphasis: MIND

Origin

This perennial climbing plant is a native of Europe and North America but is cultivated throughout the world. Hops can climb up to 8 meters (24 feet). The pollen called lupulin is strongly permeated with essential oil, and is located in the glandular hairs of the flowering heads.

Traditional Use

It is commonly known that hops possesses special properties as a treatment for insomnia. It alleviates nervous tension and neuralgic complaints, also sexual neuroses are treated with it. It augments the effect of estrogen in cases of amenorrhea. The fragrance of burning hops engenders deep relaxation and it is used for heart disease as well as stomach problems and liver complaints. Of course its significance for brewing beer should not be ignored.

Notes on Burning as Incense

Because of its intensity this valerian-like fragrant incense should only be used in very small amounts. It is added to incense mixtures as a calming and sleep promoting component. As incense the powder burns strong and fast, and it is said to enhance subtle contact with the forces of nature.

Fragrance Message

The redeeming strengths of forgiveness and balance allow painfully rigid structures to soften.

'Crossing the borders'

MARSH TEA

Ledum padesirere
Heath plant/Ericaceae
Syn.: Wild rosemary, cankerroot, ledum
Part of plant: Herbage
Elemental force: FIRE
Emphasis: BODY

Origin

This bushy heath plant grows to a maximum height of 1.5 meters (4.5 feet). It thrives in the high moors of the Nordic countries often together with pine and birch, which are common there. It is also found in Alpine regions and in cool moist areas of Asia and North America. From a purely visual perspective marsh tea is reminiscent of rosemary but it has a softer charm.

Traditional Use

In addition to juniper this is the most important plant for the Eurasian shaman with a history extending back to the Ice Age, when people rubbed it on themselves as a remedy for rheumatic complaints. They burned it as medicinal incense for whooping cough or drunk as a tea for asthma and colds. The Teutons used it as an intoxicating addition to beer (wild rosemary beer), which helped augment its aggressive effects. It has long been known as a sleep inducing incense and is also considered to be an insect repellant.

This ancient herb continues to play an important role because inhaling its consciousness altering aromatic smoke can trigger shamanic states of trance during healing rituals.

Notes on Burning as Incense

The hot character of this pleasant spicy resinous fragrance spreads a campfire atmosphere and can be wonderful when burned alone. Do not use during pregnancy!

Fragrance Message

We open gates to the primal forces of nature in order to discover which will advance the process.

*'Powerful presence
and ability to take action'*

MASTIC

Pistacia lenticus
Sumac plant/Anacardiaceae
Syn.: Mastic tree
Part of plant: Resin
Elemental force: AIR
Emphasis: MIND

Origin

This is an evergreen shrub that also grows as a tree of 3 to 4 meters (9 to 12 feet). It is found around the Mediterranean especially in hot rocky places where its many branches give off a resinous fragrance. The resin itself which it exudes in small balls is collected once it has dried and solidified. The best quality has always come from the Greek island of Chios.

Traditional Use

Mastic was chewed in antiquity for oral hygiene. Today its significance extends from perfumery to the food industry, and it's handy as an adhesive for theater beards.

As an incense mastic has been firmly established in a variety of cultures since ancient times. It is a component of many recipes ranging from kyphi to church frankincense mixtures. The basic effect of this substance is astringent and tonifying. When burned as incense it is said to promote clairvoyance and lead to visions of the supernatural.

Notes on Burning as Incense

Burning mastic helps us to wake up and concentrate. The result of this can be a cleansing and strengthening of the overall constitution. The heart opening quality of these light yellow transparent 'sun seeds', which develop their warm and resinous fragrance in the smoke, creates lightness and enjoyment.

Fragrance Message

The fog of melancholy is chased out of the heart making it possible for new trust in life to arise.

'Feeling the contact with yourself'

MUGWORT

Artemisia vulgaris
Artemisia officinalis
Composite/Asteraceae
Syn.: Maidenwort, St. John's plant
Part of plant: Herbage
Elemental force: AIR
Emphasis: BODY

Origin

This perennial strongly branched plant whose reddish stem reaches up to 1.5 meters (5 feet) grows wild and frequents all of the temperate zones around the world. It probably originated in Eastern Europe/Western Asia.

Traditional Use

Mugwort is a plant belonging to ancient cult traditions. The European use of it as incense dates back to Germanic and Celtic rituals. It is the last herb of the seasonal cycle and is offered in smoke to celebrate the summer solstice. Burning it as incense is considered protective magic against evil and danger.

The Christian epoch transformed mugwort into a witches' herb. The moxibustion of Traditional Chinese Medicine burns it on the skin as a heat stimulus for gout and rheumatism. The incense is also said to be sexually arousing and strengthening for male potency.

Notes on Burning as Incense

This herb is a *border crosser* and therefore suitable for guiding people safely past the *Guardians of the Threshold*. It can be burned as incense to accompany transformational experiences. The bittersweet fragrance has a relaxing, warming and calming effect on the nerves. It opens and prepares the way for inner composure and strength.

Fragrance Message

At the threshold the forces are concentrated and the soul is purified before we head for new shores. To do this we need a clear view of things as they really are.

'Concentrating on what is authentic'

MYRRH

Commiphora abyssinica
Balsamodendron myrrha
Balsamiferous plant/Burseraceae
Syn.: genuine Myrrh,
Arabian Myrrh
Part of plant: Resin
Elemental force: EARTH
Emphasis: EMOTION

Origin

This bushy balsam tree, which may grow to 10 meters (30 feet), is a native of north-eastern Africa and south-western Asia, predominantly in the area around the Red Sea. With an acacia like appearance it has knotted thorny twigs, fragrance exuding leaf stems bearing three leaves and small white flowers. Resin, which exudes when the bark is injured, is collected after it has hardened.

Traditional Use

There are all types of mythological stories about this famous resin. It is mentioned many times in the Bible. Myrrh is indispensable in a wide range of religious and medicinal applications. Its numbing, drying and astringent powers work against spoilage and every type of decay, which is why it was an essential component in the embalming procedures of the ancient Egyptians. It is *rejuvenating* for body and mind. The antiseptic effect of myrrh is especially strong

and its healing influence on the female genital system has been praised since antiquity.

Notes on Burning as Incense

This earthy fragrance combines beautifully with other resins to ensure grounding. Suppressed emotions become integrated since its effect also extends to the subtle bodies.

Fragrance Message

Emotional ground is prepared for the spiritual seed and the soul is nourished.

'Fertility and purity'

MYRTLE LEAVES

Myrtus communis
Myrtle tree/Myrtaceae
Syn.: Myrtle
Part of plant: Leaves
Elemental force: FIRE
Emphasis: MIND

Origin

This 3 meters (9 feet) evergreen bush or small tree loves moist lime deficient soils. It comes from northern Africa and is now propagated across the entire Mediterranean. It has shiny lance shaped leaves, delicate white flowers and small juniper like berries. The leaves and flowers contain large amounts of essential oil and have a fragrance that ranges from tart/sweet to camphor.

Traditional Use

Myrtle has always been used dried and bound for burning. It was sacred to the ancients and considered the very principle of virginal purity and grace.

Medicinally it was burned as incense for all types of pain relief. Thought also to maintain and promote youthful vitality and the ability to love in the highest sense.

Myrtle's healing qualities are valued for skin care, the respiratory tract and urinary system as well as for the immune system, fighting colds, flu and infectious diseases. It has a relaxing and harmonizing effect on the psyche.

Notes on Burning as Incense

Leafy with a peppery and fruity undertone, myrtle smoke can be integrated into mixtures with mastic and lavender to achieve a beautifully cleansing refreshing effect which is energetically balanced.

Fragrance Message

Old emotional wounds are healed when clarity expands through the act of forgiving. As a consequence beauty and love enrich the present for a happy new beginning.

'Transparency and free vision'

NARD

Nardostachys jatamansi
Valerian plant/Valerianaceae
Syn: Spikenarde/valerian
Part of plant: Root
Elemental force: EARTH
Emphasis: EMOTION

Origin

This delicate aromatic valerian grows predominantly in the Himalayas, but in the high mountains of China and Japan it is also native at heights above 3,000 meters (9,000 feet). It forms a pinkish white flower and has woody red-brown roots that exude a sharp fragrance. The dried and chopped root has been collected to extract the essential oil and to burn as incense since time immemorial.

Traditional Use

The aromatic stimulus of this root has been valued since the age of ancient Egypt. Even the *Song of Solomon* sings of the irresistible fragrance of *nard* in a passage where it is vividly equated with the feminine sex. In the medicinal sense it is also said to have a regulative effect on female cycles.

Nard has great significance in Ayurvedic recipes for the treatment of hysteria and other neurological disorders. In cases of restlessness and insomnia and for every type of overwrought state, burning it as incense can be very helpful. Nard is an important component of many incense compositions.

Notes on Burning as Incense

This fragrance can be called warming and drying with a woody/musty somewhat animalistic undertone. It sensitizes the sensory organs and strengthens body feelings with expanded consciousness.

Can be mixed well with frankincense, myrrh and myrtle.

Fragrance Message

Radiating peace and strength it puts us on the solid ground of inner reality.

'Finding the center'

NUT GRASS RHIZOME

Cyperus scariosus
Cyperus rotundus
Cypress grass plant/Cyperaceous
Syn.: Indian cypress, Tamil.: *Koraikkilangu*
Part of plant: Root
Elemental force: EARTH
Emphasis: BODY

Origin

This grass can be found in abundance in the moist tropical regions of Bengal and Uttar Pradesh as well as in the eastern and southern parts of India. Its tuberous dark root develops a strong fibrous network. Cyperus rotundus is at home in the moist regions of Egypt and was used as incense in ancient times.

Traditional Use

As an important plant in Ayurvedic medicine the root is employed as a stimulant for digestive disorders and fever. Healing compresses made of the crushed root are also applied to scorpion stings. It is fundamental to the production of Indian incense sticks and burning it can create an aphrodisiac effect and also help strengthen the memory. Some people say that nut grass rhizome palliates emotional disorders, irritability and depression.

Notes on Burning as Incense

Burning the root as incense has a relaxing and calming effect on the nerves, while stimulating the mind. The fragrance has a dark warm oriental note and lies between eaglewood, vetiver root and nard. It gives any mixture an earthy base.

Fragrance Message

The supportive foundation creates community and allows an opening toward all sides.

'Strength from the center'

NUTMEG

Myristica fragrans
Nux moschata
Nutmeg plant/Myristicaceae
Syn: Nutmeg
Part of plant: Seed
Elemental force: FIRE
Emphasis: BODY

Origin

This evergreen tree grows to a height of 20 meters (60 feet) and comes from the Moluccas. Today it is cultivated in India, Indonesia (East Indies) and the Caribbean (West Indies). Nutmeg, the dried seeds from the fleshy fruit, is ground for use. The flowers, mace flowers, are also dried and have similar properties to nutmeg.

Traditional Use

Known worldwide primarily as an indispensable kitchen spice, nutmeg is also used medicinally as a remedy for digestive disorders, kidney ailments and rheumatism. It has a stimulating and tonifying effect on the nervous system, and aphrodisiac qualities are also attributed to it. Myristicin, one of the main components of the essential oil, has hallucinogenic effects on the cerebral cortex which is connected with motor activity.

'Less is more' also applies to burning this spice which according to occult schools has significance in promoting contact at spiritualist sessions. It is also burned to bring happiness and as protection from negative influences.

Notes on Burning as Incense

Burning nutmeg as incense strengthens the power of the self and helps remedy indecisiveness.

Fragrance Message

Your will is your heavenly kingdom and where there is a will there is also a way.

'Everything is possible'

OAKMOSS

Evernia prunastri
Lichen plant/Usneaceae
Syn.: Evernia
Part of plant: Lichen
Elemental force: EARTH
Emphasis: BODY

Origin

Growing on a great variety of trees it is collected, preferably from oak in Europe, particularly in France, the Balkan countries and Greece. It also comes from Morocco, Algeria and North America.

Lichen are hermaphroditic beings. At the dawn of time algae and fungus as pioneers of life entered into a symbiosis so as to complete the conquest of the continents. They produce for example an acid with whose help stone can be transformed over time into rich soil.

Traditional Use

Native Americans traditionally use oakmoss as a remedy for respiratory complaints and the British plant pharmacopoeia also lists it for these. It is recommended especially for bronchitis, coughs and asthma in children and is said to have a soothing effect.

Notes on Burning as Incense

The bitter leathery/warm 'primal fragrance' of this lichen is very intense. It represents the past, processes left behind, like the suffering through which we must all pass and as such can thereby support and stimulate the resolution of painful memories. Oakmoss ideally suited to occasions that involve a letting go hence it is a substance especially appropriate to burn in the presence of someone who is dying.

Fragrance Message

Solid ground that gives security and strengthens self-confidence.

'Everything is one'

OPOPONAX

Commiphora erythraea
Balsamiferous plant/Burseraceae
Syn.: Pastinaca opoponax, sweet myrrh
Part of plant: Herbage
Elemental force: FIRE
Emphasis: EMOTION

Origin

Genuine opoponax chironicum comes from an umbellated plant which is rarely available today. Commiphora erythraea is a large tropical tree similar to myrrh that is a native of Ethiopia and Somalia. For the harvest of raw gum the trunk is scarified and the exuded gum resin collected after it has dried to a dark red-brown lump.

Traditional Use

Since its effects are very similar to those of genuine myrrh, opoponax is an important component of incense produced in the Middle East. It is also burned to disinfect houses and protect from negative influences. In perfumery, oil distilled from this resin serves as a high quality fixing agent. As a flavoring it lends liqueurs a taste similar that of to wine.

Notes on Burning as Incense

A mysterious smell like the soothing woody/sweet fragrance of old wine corks, opoponax is very relaxing and strengthening to the senses as an incense. It promotes inspiration, intuitive perception and optimism.

Fragrance Message

Deep wishes are revealed in a harmoniously balanced atmosphere and may then be entrusted to the flow of life. The pain of the past dissolves.

'Completely in the here and now'

PALO SANTO

Bursera graveolens
Balsamiferous plant/Burseraceae
Part of plant: Wood
Elemental force: FIRE
Emphasis: EMOTION

Origin

This bushy balsam tree, which grows to a maximum of 15 meters (45 feet), with its many small branches looks a bit like the Arabian frankincense tree. It is said to have its origins on the Islands of Santa Cruz and Galapagos, and is known to have been a native of Peru for thousands of years. It is a source of South American copal and its resinous wood can be burned as a wonderful incense.

Traditional Use

Copalcoahuitl is the name given by the Aztecs to all aromatic balsamiferous plants that give off richly scented incense fragrance. Thus Indian copal became the classic frankincense of Meso-American indigenous peoples. For the Indians of Peru traditional use of palo santo (= holy wood) for medicinal, religious and magical ritual purposes goes back thousands of years. It is said that while evil spirits avoid this fragrance the good spirits are drawn to it.

Palo santo still has many uses today to support healing and to cleanse the air.

Notes on Burning as Incense

The warm/aromatic, tart/woody smoke of smoldering splinters of copal creates peace and harmony and lays down an optimistic mood. This is an ideal incense to relax irritation and tension.

Fragrance Message

Quiet joy spreads when all burdens dissolve as they burn away and fly out the window.

'Allowing the heart to become lighter'

PATCHOULI

Pogostemon patchouli
Pogostemon cablin
Labiate/Lamiaceae
Syn.: Patchouli, Ind. *Patch Pan*
Part of plant: Herbage
Elemental force: EARTH
Emphasis: BODY

Origin

Native of Malaysia, the Philippines and Indonesia this famous representative of the menthaceous (mint) family is now cultivated in China, India, Australia, Madagascar and Paraguay. The plant loves a moist warm climate with fertile soil and attains a height of 1 meter (3 feet). Its leaves, which are 6 to 8 cm long (2.5 to 3 inches), are odorless when fresh. The well-known smell of patchouli only develops after harvest through a process of fermentation.

Traditional Use

Patchouli is primarily cultivated for the extraction of its essential oil which is valued throughout the world for its medicinal effect on the skin.

It is anti-inflammatory, vitalizing and powerful for the body while calming, balancing and mood brightening for the psyche. Its sensual/erotic quality and excellence as a fixative make this plant important in perfumery.

As a moth repellant it is valuable in the home. For this purpose and to get rid of bad smells it is burned as incense.

Notes on Burning as Incense

The incense fragrance is dark and earthy like black, fertile, fermenting soil or an old potato storage cellar. This substance represents deep grounding, offers strength, expels fear and blends well into any sensuous incense composition.

Fragrance Message

This is the impulse of basic security in our physical existence which allows us to release what is old.

'Basic trust and a strong presence'

PINE RESIN

Pinus sylvestris
Pine family/Pinaceae
Syn.: Colophonium (rosin), colophony
Part of plant: Resin
Elemental force: AIR
Emphasis: MIND

Origin

This evergreen conifer achieves a height of 40 meters (120 feet), has a flat crown, reddish-black bark and long needles that form in pairs. It has the tendency to grow in marginal areas as it is modest in its demands. It is cultivated in Russia and the USA but is native to all of Europe. Resin exudes from cracks in the bark and can be collected throughout the entire year. Colophonium (rosin) is distilled from pine balm. In this process the water residue is evaporated giving it a golden glassy appearance.

Traditional Use

Dating as far back as the old Teutonic tree cult, pine was considered a symbol of endurance and the capacity to survive. Its resin was called 'forest frankincense' due to the calm and peace it induces. In German folklore it was seen as a protective force against negative influences and witchcraft. Medicinally pine is used for strengthening the lungs, as a germicidal and

as a tonic. A powerful and warming effect is attributed to burning the resin as incense. It energizes the body, relaxes the mind and creates joy in the heart.

Notes on Burning as Incense

The relation between body and mind (Saturn-Mercury) is strengthened. Constricted states are dissolved in the air and into expansiveness. Use with caution on a sieve!

Fragrance Message

When things get tight and the path becomes steep strength and confidence come with a deep breath … and we continue.

'Staying in the game'

ROSE FLOWERS

Pink damascena
Rose family/Rosaceae
Syn.: Turkish rose
Part of plant: Petals
Elemental force: WATER
Emphasis: EMOTION

Origin

This oriental species of rose is mainly cultivated in Bulgaria, Turkey and France although there are similar types growing in China, Russia and India. A small thorny bush that grows 1 to 2 meters (3 to 6 feet), it has many full pink flowers of 3 to 5 cm in diameter (1 to 2 inches) and develops a strong fragrance.

Traditional Use

The oil of this rose is used to cool down over heated conditions and has a soothing effect on injuries. States of anxiety and stagnant energy may be stimulated by Turkish rose. It is also known for its aphrodisiac powers. The fragrance has a calming and relaxing effect on nervous conditions of stress and insomnia.

Notes on Burning as Incense

Burning rose flowers as incense can be supporting when we seek self-acceptance and wish to let go of prejudices. A fragrance which allows opening and loving contact to arise. The only satisfactory way to burn rose flowers is on a sieve, where they can burn more slowly than directly on the hot coals. They also work well with sandalwood and various resins. Rose flowers contribute a delicate flowery sensuousness to aromatic mixtures, and have a healing effect on emotional injuries of the heart.

Fragrance Message

A waft of warmth and gentle kindness allows all quarrels and anger to be forgotten.

'Understanding and forgiving'

R O S E M A R Y

ROSEMARY

Rosemarinus officinalis
Labiate/Lamiaceae
Syn.: Rosemary
Part of plant: Leaves
Elemental force: FIRE
Emphasis: MIND

Origin

Originally a native of the Mediterranean this 1 to 2 meter (3 to 6 feet) evergreen bush is now also cultivated in many other European countries, in the US, Russia, the Near East and in China. With its luxuriant, proliferating foliage of leathery needle-like leaves it sometimes develops bizarre shapes.

Traditional Use

This plant turns up everywhere from cosmetics and cuisine to a wide range of healing arts. Whether consecrating sacred sites in Ancient Greece, driving away evil spirits and the plague during the Middle Ages, or dealing with diverse health disorders ranging from those of the respiratory tract to the circulation, liver, digestion, hair growth, muscle pain or neuralgia, rosemary's broad spectrum of effectiveness has always been called upon.

Notes on Burning as Incense

A hot spicy fragrance familiar to many people, rosemary is an excellent conclusion to an incense burning ritual. It is 'a bush that tries to be a tree' (Martin Henglein) and thereby embodies an energetic thrust for every process.

Fragrance Message

A matter of consciously stepping into change and perceiving the spiritual impulse. Both consciousness and mental powers are strengthened to take action rather than stagnate.

'Taking action'

SAGE

Salvia officinalis
Labiate/Lamiaceae
Syn.: Salvia, garden sage, red sage
Part of plant: Leaves
Elemental force: AIR
Emphasis: BODY

Origin

The home of *herba sacra* (= the sacred herb) as the Romans called it is the entire Mediterranean region. It is an evergreen bushy shrub that can grow to a height of 80 cm (32 inches). The woody base continually produces young shoots from which the glistening silvery, elongated oval leaves develop many blue to violet groups of blossoms.

Traditional Use

The name (*salvare* = healing) already suggests the potency of this plant. As a highly effective remedy for many ailments ranging from inflammations in the mouth and throat to the respiratory tract, it has always been widely used. In the field of sacred mysticism it is considered extremely effective in warding off demons and spirits. Its influence on the mind ranges from improving the memory to relieving disturbing emotions. In Ayurveda sage is classified as a mood altering remedy with the capacity to stimulate the mind.

Notes on Burning as Incense

The resinous aromatic freshness of this smoke brings clarity, neutrality and cleanliness into a room. Burning sage subdues the passions, which makes it an outstanding ritual incense for meditation.

Fragrance Message

Shielding against wrong so that peace and quiet can arise.

Health, strength and long life

SAGE-WHITE

Salvia apiana
Labiate/Lamiaceae
Syn.: White sage
California White Sage
Part of plant: Herbage
Elemental force: WATER
Emphasis: BODY

Origin

White sage grows in hot sunny places along the Southern Californian coastline especially between Santa Barbara and the Baja peninsula. It grows to a height of 60 to 90 cm (24 to 36 inches) and the leaves are a frosted silver green that is velvety to the touch. It sprouts a panicle with light blue flowers. The abundant seeds serve both humans and animals as food.

Traditional Use

Medicinally white sage is considered to be tonifying, antiseptic and fever reducing. Brewed as a tea it has a calming effect. The leaves can also be chewed to eliminate bad breath. Among other things the Native American medicine man adds this sage to smoke mixtures for the relief of asthma and lung complaints.

For Native Americans white sage is an important ritual incense. Burned this way a strong and calming healing force may come to unfold. This makes it an outstanding compliment to prayer and peace ceremonies as it encourages the willingness to negotiate. Its cleansing powers are especially called upon for sweatlodge ceremonies. It has a cooling nature.

Notes on Burning as Incense

The intense aromatic fragrance is highly recommended for cleansing and attuning the self to ritual body and trance work.

Fragrance Message

Making wise decisions with a clear mind.

Looking at what is essential

135

SANDALWOOD-RED

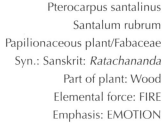

Pterocarpus santalinus
Santalum rubrum
Papilionaceous plant/Fabaceae
Syn.: Sanskrit: *Ratachananda*
Part of plant: Wood
Elemental force: FIRE
Emphasis: EMOTION

Origin

This small tree, which never reaches 10 meters (30 feet), grows mainly in India and Sri Lanka. Mentioned in the Bible* its wood was also used to build temples and places worship in ancient Palestine.

Traditional Use

The Ayurvedic teachings consider red sandalwood to be the brother of white sandalwood and attribute similar properties to it even though they have no botanical relationship. The emphasis of its effect tends to be more in the external world (Leo principle) however. The red color of the wood signals its aphrodisiac quality. The wood is also used for the extraction and production of natural dye which is added to incense to improve its appearance.

Notes on Burning as Incense

The smoke of red sandalwood has a warm and delicate/aromatic woody fragrance. Because of its own subtle note it is very suitable as a carrier for all types of fragrant compositions. Recommended for incense mixtures together with balsams such as styrax Honduras as well as various resins like benzoin and copal.

Fragrance Message

When beauty occurs in appearance, expression can become the medium of strength and lead to perfection.

'Serving in love'

SANDALWOOD-WHITE

Santalum album
Thesium plant/Santalaceae
Syn.: Eastern Indian sandalwood;
sandalwood
Part of plant: Wood
Elemental force: EARTH
Emphasis: EMOTION

Origin

The home of this evergreen tree, which can grow up to 12 meters (36 feet), is Southeast Asia and especially the Indian province of Mysore. It is a semi-parasite that thrives on the roots of bamboo and certain species of palm from which it supplies itself with nutrients (nitrogen and phosphorus). The very hard wood takes 20 years to develop the desired fragrance which arises when it is dried.

Traditional Use

For thousands of years the fragrance of white sandalwood has been a part of cultural and religious practices throughout the entire world. It is still an indispensable component for the world of perfume. Mixing well with almost every other fragrance it also serves as a fixative.

Medicinally it is considered cooling, germicidal and neutralizing. Used as a remedy for inflammation and respiratory diseases, it also relieves nausea and nervous tensions. For the people of India sandalwood is an aid in the transition into a higher reincarnation. It opens the energy channel to the forces of the earth, transforms fear and clears the way to the source of inner strength.

Notes on Burning as Incense

When this incense is burned the fragrance is warm, soothing and gentle. It is outstandingly well suited to all types of mixtures. Egoism in the body is subdued and an atmosphere of peace and self-communion is created.

Fragrance Message

We should be in our center and feel that we are a part of the Greater Whole. It is best to devote ourselves to the current of life with trust and love.

The supportive foundation

137

SANDARAC

Tetraclinis articulata
Cypress plant/Cupressaceae
Syn.: Berber thuja,
Part of plant: Resin
Elemental force: FIRE
Emphasis: BODY

Origin

The sandarac tree is a native of northern Africa, particularly Morocco and south-eastern Spain in hot dry regions. It can attain a height of 15 meters (45 feet) and has a dark redish/brown wood. It belongs to the family of the thujas and the extended family of white cedar. Golden yellow stalactite-like drops of resin with a powdery surface and glassy shiny fractures are scratched off the trunk and branches some days after scarification.

Traditional Use

This tree was already being cultivated by the Romans at the edge of the Sahara for its resin which they used as incense. The beautiful texturing of its root wood is still sought after for finely crafted fragrant wooden objects. In North African folk medicine this resin plays an important role as an antispasmodic for difficult births as well as for digestive disorders, head colds and catarrh. It is used as a cleansing incense to clear the atmosphere in homes.

Notes on Burning as Incense

The warm resinous fragrance with its velvety/fresh undertone has a distinctly relaxing effect on the autonomic nervous system and is well suited to mixtures including benzoin, cedar, sandalwood and angelica root for a pleasant evening burn.

Fragrance Message

An inner connection with the whole allows energy to flow freely and clears all obstacles out of the way.

'Clarity of the pure heart'

SIAM BENZOIN

Styrax tonkinensis
Anthostyrax tonkinensis
Styrax tree/Styraceae
Syn.: Siam Snowbell
Part of plant: Resin
Elemental force: WATER
Emphasis: EMOTION

Origin

The styrax tree, which grows up to 20 meters (65 feet) and has thin chocolate colored bark, is native to Laos, Vietnam, Thailand, Malaysia and Cambodia. The bark is scarified down to the wood and when it turns a reddish-brown color the exuded secretion is harvested as benzoin resin.

It is very fragile and whitish at the point of fracture before the air turns it golden brown.

Traditional Use

This is one of the most important incense substance there is in Asia. It is part of almost every type of incense stick and has been imported into Europe since the 15th century. Medicinally it was mostly used externally as a tincture to relieve eczema, fungal/parasitic growth, to treat wounds (wound balm). Only occasionally was it taken internally, as an expectorant. Even the ancient Egyptians considered benzoin to be a valuable ingredient of ointments, perfume and incense.

The titillating seductive aspect of benzoin lends the incense an aphrodisiac quality for sensuous occasions.

Notes on Burning as Incense

It is advisable to burn benzoin in incense mixtures together with for instance: sandalwood, eaglewood, frankincense, myrrh, labdanum or tonka bean. Burned alone it initially has a very sharp smell and almost takes your breath away before the balsamic vanilla like aroma arises.

Fragrance Message

The feelings are healed in a gentle way so that protectively and helpfully, spiritual power can develop.

'Soothing for the wounded soul'

139

SPRUCE RESIN

Picea abies
Pine tree/Pinaceae
Syn.: Spruce rosin, pine resin,
Burgundy resin
Part of plant: Resin
Elemental force: AIR
Emphasis: BODY

Origin

The spruce is common in Europe. It grows to a height of 50 to 70 meters (150 to 210 feet) and is shallow rooted. Its fast growing wood and very straight trunk have lent it a wide range of industrial uses, hence large areas have been planted as monoculture. The abundantly available resin is refined through a heating process and sold under the name of Burgundy resin.

Traditional Use

As a holy tree of the Teutons the spruce represented protection and healing (mother tree), and was used to help overcome the trauma of dying as 'the victory of the spirit of light beyond death.'*

The disinfecting strength of spruce resin incense was already valued in ancient times for cleansing rooms. It is also said to be an expectorant and effective for gout and rheumatism. Turpentine is derived from spruce resin.

When it is burned as incense it has an intoxicating effect that is both euphoric and numbing. Because this could be detrimental to health it should in no way be overdone.

Notes on Burning as Incense

The intense woodsy dark green fragrance created by burning spruce resin as incense can be used for restorative and strengthening purposes. Be cautious when burning it on the sieve because it melts and easily becomes runny and is very combustible.

Fragrance Message

Heaven and earth are connected and the body integrates itself and mediates in the service of Creation.

Passing on the light

* S. Fischer-Rizzi, *Blätter von Bäumen*, Irsiana, Munich, 1998, pages 81ff.

STAR ANISE

Illicum verum
Magnolia tree/Illiceaceae
Syn.: Shikimi tree, badian pepper
Part of plant: Resin
Elemental force: WATER
Emphasis: EMOTION

Origin

This evergreen tree with its slender white trunk can grow to a height of 14 meters (42 feet). It is cultivated throughout Asia. The yellow flowers are similar to narcissus and its fruit consists of 5–10 seed chambers in a star shape around a central axis. They can be harvested twice a year.

Traditional Use

Star anise is valued as a traditional component featuring in a great many Asian incense preparations. It is indispensable in Japanese incense sticks. Burned to repel fleas and body lice, it has also a traditional place as a kitchen spice in Chinese cuisine. The fragrance reminds of Christmas. In medicinal terms star anise is considered pain relieving and an expectorant for coughs. It also alleviates stomach cramps, bad breath and rheumatism. In Western occultism the use of this incense is said to increase psychic powers. An aphrodisiac and harmonizing effect on the nervous system is also attributed to it. Heavy use can trigger a mildly narcotic effect.

Notes on Burning as Incense

Star anise combines easily with cinnamon, fennel, cloves and sandalwood to make a very relaxing incense. Avoid over use.

Fragrance Message

The needy shall be soothed and comforted. We will receive motherly care and nourishment.

'Let yourself fall and trust'

STYRAX

Styrax calamitus
Liquidambar officinalis
Hamamelis plant/Hamamelidaceae
Syn.: Storax, liquid amber
Part of plant: Resinoid
Elemental force: WATER
Emphasis: EMOTION

Origin

The balsam of the bushy styrax tree, which grows up to 10 meters (30 feet) has the consistency and color of viscous honey, hence 'liquid amber'. Asia Minor is the home of the classic amber tree. South East Asia and Central America are two areas where styrax is traditionally extracted. A customary way of burning this sticky substance as incense is to drench coal chips in styrax. This is practical and unproblematic. Unfortunately the authenticity of the substance cannot always be guaranteed.

Traditional Use

Styrax is a traditional incense whose history goes back into ancient times. It features in many mythological stories and experts think that it is the 'Balm of Gilead' mentioned in the Bible.

In medicinal terms it is considered effective as treatment for respiratory diseases, and Dioscurides also reports on its softening, digestive powers. In ancient times it was offered to the female deity Hecate as a cultic incense with magical powers. It was also used along with Syrian rue and bay as an oracle incense*.

Notes on Burning as Incense

Deeply relaxing and relieving for emotional spasms, burning styrax can work wonders when aggression dominates a situation. Its subsequent fragrance spreads the soothing gentle sweetness of serenity.

Fragrance Message

A mood of openness breezes through the heart, offering a chance to make dreams come true.

'Use this special moment'

SUGANDHA KOKILA

Cinnamomum cecidodaphne
Cinnamomum glaucescents
Bay plant/Lauraceae
Syn.: "Fragrant Cuckoo,"
Gondserai, Nepal: *Mallagiri*
Part of plant: Fruit
Elemental force: FIRE
Emphasis: BODY

Origin

This large evergreen tree can be found in the wilds of the eastern Himalayas primarily in Nepal but also in Sikkim, Bhutan, Assam and Sylhet at elevations up to 1,300 meters (3,900 feet). It grows very quickly, reaching a height of about 7 meters (21 feet). Its cork-like fragrant bark is used commercially along with the enormous quantity of small (3 cm/1.5 inches) fruit that it produces.

Traditional Use

The wood of this tree is also called Nepal camphor or Nepal sassafras. It is extremely water and insect resistant and is also used to repel vermin. A very popular wood, it is useful in furniture production and shipbuilding. In Ayurveda the fruit is considered restorative and stimulating and the essential oil is classified as a fungicide

Notes on Burning as Incense

The fragrance of the crushed fruit, similar to a combination of cinnamon, clove and eucalyptus is quite peculiar and not very pleasant when burned alone. The psychic effect is stimulating, polarizing the emotions. In activating incense mixtures (such as those with dammar and juniper) the desired effect may be intensified with a pleasant unfolding of fragrance.

Fragrance Message

When laziness takes over and boredom sets in, this calls for change.

'Will to action and assertiveness'

SUNSET HIBISCUS SEEDS

Hibiscus abelmoschus
Mallow plant/Malvaceae
Syn.: Okra; Ambrette seed
Part of plant: Seed
Elemental force: WATER
Emphasis: EMOTION

Origin

This annual plant with crème-yellow flowers resembling hibiscus can grow to a height of 1.25 meters (4 feet). It is cultivated in most tropical countries but especially in Ecuador, Columbia and India, where its also grown for the green pods, known as okra, that are eaten as a vegetable. The seed ripens later in these pods.

Traditional Use

Okra seeds are roasted as a coffee substitute and the food industry uses the oil to add an attractive aroma to liqueurs. For perfume production 'ambrette oil' is distilled from the seed and herbage and integrated into flowery scents along with tones of chypre and wood. Some find it exhilarating. It is energizing and stimulating where a lack of sex drive is a problem, also easing nerve cramps. Burned as incense the sunset hibiscus seeds develop a profoundly dark/sweet to burnt smelling musk-like fragrance that is somewhat reminiscent of tobacco and cognac. It is also said to have an erotic effect.

Notes on Burning as Incense

The incense creates both tension and grounding, so that instinctual emotional energy can be expressed though the body and control relinquished.

Fragrance Message

Opening up to everything that is available and dreaming of beauty.

'Feeling who you are.'

SWEET GRASS

Hierochloe odorata
Savastana odorata
Sweetgrasses/Poaceae
Syn.: Vanilla grass, Seneca grass,
holy grass
Part of plant: Herbage
Elemental force: WATER
Emphasis: EMOTION

Origin

This fragrant grass shrub from the North American prairies loves moist hollows and grows about 90 cm tall (36 inches). It is closely related to the European sweet vernal grass *(Anthoxantum odoratum),* which is found in meadows and along waysides. Native Americans cut sweet grass, braid it and dry it for incense.

Traditional Use

In Native American spiritual life sweet grass is considered an important 'power plant'. Traditionally a medicinal tea for colds and abdominal pain, as well as fragrant jewelry for ritual occasions, its main importance is as incense although it is often also added to tobacco mixtures. Sweet grass is always used when the good, beauty and lightness of life are being sought as an offering. In the sweatlodge cleansing ceremony it is said to encourage good spirits to participate.

Notes on Burning as Incense

The delicate vanilla like fragrance of a sweet grass burning is reminiscent of fresh hay and sweet woodruff. Perfect to create a friendly cheerful atmosphere. It is well combined with white sage or copal resin to strengthen a cleansing effect.

Fragrance Message

This is a friendly greeting, a loving gesture and a happy smile.

'Entering into harmony'

SYRIAN RUE

Peganum harmala L.
Zygophyllaceae
Syn.: Harmel, wild rue, Syrian rue
Part of plant: Seed
Elemental force: AIR
Emphasis: EMOTION

Origin

This bushy herbaceous plant grows up to 1 meter (3 feet) and is at home in desert regions from Western Asia to northern India, Mongolia and Manchuria. Narrow pinnate leaf segments produce small white flowers in the branch axils. The fruit hides many small square seeds which have an anesthetizing fragrance, and contain hallucinogenic substances.

Traditional Use

Wherever this plant thrives it is highly reputed in local folk medicine. We can assume this relates to its shamanic use in magical/spiritual healing rituals. The Dervishes in Buchara also use *harmel* in healing ceremonies. In Morocco the seeds are burned as incense in clay containers on glowing coals to ward off bad luck. When inhaled deeply the smoke is said to create ecstatic states that make visions possible. A light burning of this incense is said to lend clarity and relaxation to the spirit, for example to assist in childbirth. Indian folk medicine classifies Syrian rue as an aphrodisiac.

Notes on Burning as Incense

This tart burnt-smelling fragrance is easy to tolerate. If not ground in advance the seed kernels burst with a discreet bang. Together with coriander it has an especially mood-brightening quality.

Fragrance Message

Be connected with everything and able to trustingly open yourself.

The seeker is guided to the light

TEJPAT

Cinnamomum tamala
Cinnamomum iners
Bay plant/Lauraceae
Syn.: Tamalpatri, tejput,
Tam. *Talishappattiri*
Part of plant: Leaves
Elemental force: FIRE
Emphasis: BODY

Origin

Related to the cinnamon family this evergreen tree can be found in the tropics and subtropics of northern India, the Himalayas up to an elevation of 2,500 meters (7,500 feet) and also Burma. Its bark and leaves are used medicinally.

Traditional Use

The bark is often substituted for Ceylon cinnamon even though the fragrance is completely different. The leaves contain a great deal of eugenol and cinnamonaldehyde and are known to be a powerful stimulant. Tejpat is used as a medicine for coughs and fever and added as a spice to food to prevent flatulence and digestive disorders. Good results have been achieved in the treatment of diabetes mellitus. Because of their pleasant fragrance and stimulating effect the leaves are also burned as incense.

Notes on Burning as Incense

In stimulating incense mixes crushed leaves can be combined well with resins. The fragrance is green, powerfully spicy and allows the energy level to rise.

Fragrance Message

A provocative mood that calls us to do the things that need to be done.

'Setting off to new deeds'

TOLU BALSAM

Myroxylon balsamum
Toluifera balsamum
Papilionaceous plant/Fabaceae
Syn.: Balsam of tolu,
balsamum Americanum
Part of plant: Resin
Elemental force: WATER
Emphasis: EMOTION

Origin

This straight, handsome tropical tree can reach 20 meters (60 feet) or more. It exudes an aromatic fragrance and is very similar to the Peru balsam tree. Tolu is native to Venezuela, El Salvador, Columbia and Cuba and it is also cultivated on the islands of the West Indies. The trunk is cut in a V shape and the golden yellow viscous resin flows out and is caught in gourds. At lower temperatures it solidifies into a shiny brown paste that can easily be cracked.

Traditional Use

In Native American folk medicine tolu balsam is burned as incense for respiratory diseases, headaches and rheumatism, while in Western medicine it is used as an expectorant in cough syrup. But mostly tolu is processed as a healing and protective component in skin ointments. The Incas as said to have used it for embalming their high ranking officials. Burning tolu balsam is recommended to bring harmony during meditations and ceremonies, or as an evening incense.

Notes on Burning as Incense

In the first moment the smell can be sharp to burning but as it proceeds it becomes very sweet like vanilla. Tolu should not be burned alone on the sieve since it becomes very liquid. Very good in relaxing mixtures.

Fragrance Message

Attend to the area where something should be united in order to process emotional trauma.

'Comfort and healing'

TONKA BEAN

Dipteryx odorata
Coumarouna odorata
Papilionaceous plant/Fabaceae
Syn.: *Cumaru, dypteryx odorata*
Part of plant: Seed
Elemental force: WATER
Emphasis: EMOTION

Origin

The tonka tree which grows up to 25 meters (75 feet) is a native of northern South America: Guyana (Orinoco headwater region), Brazil and British Guiana. It has large elliptical leaves and bears a profusion of violet flowers. Today it is cultivated primarily in Venezuela and Nigeria. The seed—the tonka bean—contains glycoside bound cumarin. To release it the beans are soaked in rum for 24 hours and then dried. This triggers a fermentation process after which the cumarin level may be as much as 10%.

Traditional Use

The word *tonka* comes from the indigenous people of French Guyana where the tonka bean was presumably smoked as a narcotic. It is considered to be a cardiac stimulant, febrifuge, narcotic and an appetizer. Perfumery employs tonka oil as a fixing agent and it is also used in the food industry to disguise less pleasant smells or tastes, such as that of castor oil. Tonka is also used as an insecticide.

Notes on Burning as Incense

Tonka beans have a very intense, sweet/spicy aroma that is reminiscent of both sweet woodruff and vanilla. When burned as incense it has an anti-depressive and euphoric effect however its intensity can easily become overpowering.

Fragrance Message

Cheerful serenity arises out of warm hearted openness when the right balance is maintained.

'Enjoy and relax'

TULSI

Ocimum sanctum L.
Ocimum tenuiflorum L.
Labiate plant/
Lamiaceae (Labiatae)
Syn.: Indian basil, tulsi
Part of plant: Herbage
Elemental force: AIR
Emphasis: MIND

Origin

This important medicinal plant of the Hindus is found everywhere in northern India and Nepal, planted around most temples. It is a branched annual herb of 30 to 60 cm (12 to 24 inches) in height and is of major economic value.

Traditional Use

Tulsi has traditionally been used as a significant remedy, with pain relieving and digestive effects as well as for the treatment of malaria, respiratory diseases and insect bites. Perhaps more importantly it is revered in rituals as a religious and spiritual plant, offered to the deities Vishnu and Lakshmi. Health, happiness, prosperity and virtue are the qualities prayed for when it is burned as incense. It is also attributed to have a strong protective function when darkness prevails and negative forces threaten. Every Hindu household has its tulsi plant.

Notes on Burning as Incense

The fragrance tends to be pungent with a burnt smell. Becoming aware of unconscious processes may be the intention that needs strengthening. This incense can bequeath a pure aura, strengthening powers of resistance.

Fragrance Message

Turning toward the light and becoming conscious this force opens heart and mind.

'Loving receptiveness'

VERVAIN

Verbena officinalis
Vervain plant/Verbenaceae
Syn.: Holy herb, horse-whip
Part of plant: Herbage
Elemental force: AIR
Emphasis: MIND

Origin

This perennial plant with its short roots grows all over Europe attaining a height of 50 to 70 cm (20 to 28 inches). Small blue-white flowers sit on a partially woody base with dentate and pinnate leaves and very long stalks.

Traditional Use

Vervain is one of the twelve magic plants of the Rosicrucians. Also a sacred plant of the Celts, it ensures the perpetuation of divine inspiration and clairvoyance. It has always been applied as a powerful remedy for epilepsy, headaches and goiter, and is also said to drive off black magic and ghosts.

The Druids used vervain for fortune telling and prophecy. It's known as a witches' herb and has a special relationship to the planet Venus, strengthening the power to love. Helps fear and insecurity to vanish.

Notes on Burning as Incense

Vervain can be used as an addition to incense mixtures intended for cleansing of negative thought forms and in striving for courage and inner strength. Combines very well with frankincense and is also recommended as an outstanding protective incense. During the ritual we can visualize the resolving and accelerating effect of Mercury as well as the loving comforting effect of Venus.

Fragrance Message

When emotional outbursts have only left exhaustion and doubt in their wake, magically, here comes resolving energy.

'Healing visions from the beyond'

VETIVER

Vetiveria zizanoides
Andropogon muricatus
Grass plant/Poaceae
Syn.: Khus-khus
Part of plant: Root
Elemental force: EARTH
Emphasis: BODY

Origin

A bunch grass with straight blades and long narrow leaves, vetiver comes from southern India, Indonesia and Sri Lanka, but is now cultivated in many other parts of the world. It develops an extensive light root system and, among other things, serves to protect the soil from erosion.

Traditional Use

Since ancient times the root has been highly prized for its fine fragrance. Even today natives of these areas braid it into mats to keep out vermin and to create a pleasant aroma in the house. Vetiver has a calming and releasing effect in states of weakness and depression, nervous tension and the like. It is used in spiritual *dhoops* and Ayurvedic incense recipes for detoxification, and is known as the "fragrance of the regenerating earth." For problems related to aging it serves as a restorative tonic and cardiac. It is also known as an aphrodisiac and is burned as incense for all types of sacred ceremonies.

Notes on Burning as Incense

Vetiver combines well with sandalwood, opoponax and benzoin. It is smoky/woody/earthy with a tart undertone and can be used in meditation mixtures to increase awareness of the body.

Fragrance Message

When the long awaited rain falls on parched earth there is the smell of new life.

Accepting and loving yourself

YERBA SANTA

Eriodictyon californicum
Waterleaf plant/Hydrophyllaceae
Syn.: Mountain balm, bear plant
Part of plant: Herbage
Elemental force: AIR
Emphasis: BODY

Origin

This evergreen bushy herb, which grows to 60 to 120 cm (24 to 48 inches), thrives mainly in California where it prefers the company of redwood and Joshua trees. It can however also be found in the mountains from southern Utah to Arizona and New Mexico. It has shiny hairy, lance shaped leaves and whitish blue or lilac flowers that bloom in clusters of 6 to 10.

Traditional Use

Yerba Santa means 'holy herb' in Spanish and this is a very significant medicinal herb. Native Americans are familiar with its healing effect as an incense for colds, rheumatism, asthma and pneumonia. Crushed leaves are placed or rubbed on painful areas, chewed to relieve thirst or used in steam baths. Its fragrance is said to have great healing powers, eliminating the false concepts on which physical illnesses are based. As a result, hidden fears and the consequences of emotional trauma are expressed through the body, developing new trust from which an inner strength may then grow. A powerful protection against psychic toxins.

Notes on Burning as Incense

The fragrance is herbal and somewhat resinous. Yerba santa is a very good combining element in incense mixes. Use small amounts with great respect!

Fragrance Message

Pure and consecrated life's longing for itself unfolds deeply within us, resolving inhibiting defensive attitudes.

'Feeling love for yourself'

ZANTHOXYLUM

Zantoxylum alatum
Xantoxylum fraxineum
Rutaceous plant/Rutaceae
Syn.: Yellowwood, gopherwood
Part of plant: Fruit
Elemental force: FIRE
Emphasis: MIND

Origin

This large bush/tree grows mainly in the hot subtropical valleys of the Himalayas, Trans-Indus and Punjab. It is found along the entire foothills of the Himalayas running east as far as Bhutan. However it can also be found up to an elevation of 2000 meters (6,000 feet). Reaching a height of 4 meters (12 feet) it needs plenty of sunshine even though it tolerates temperatures down to –4°F.

Traditional Use

Medicinally the fruit and bark of this tree are equally used to stimulate the nervous system, for states of exhaustion, fever and disorders of the heart and digestive system (even for cholera).

In Ayurveda it is considered an alterative remedy. The fruit is said to be even more active and cramp relieving than the bark. It is used to relieve toothache and in Nepal as an oral hygiene agent.

Notes on Burning as Incense

The aromatic components (including aldehyde) possess a fresh/fruity citrus-like tone. This quality makes zanthoxylum suitable as a morning incense or for occasions that require an active enterprising approach. Can be combined well with resins.

Fragrance Message

Approaching life with provocatively cheerful extravagance and being open for all extremes.

'Cheerfulness and assertiveness'

Botanical Index

Botanical Name	Substance Name	Botanical Name	Substance Name
Acacia senegal Willd.	Gum Arabic, kordo-fan gum	Humulus lupulus	Lupulin, hops
Acorus calamus	Calamus root, flag-root	Illicum verum	Star anise
		Inula helenium	Inula
Alpinia galanga	Galangal	Juniperus communis	Juniper berries, malmot berries
Angelica archangelica	Angelica root		
Aquillaria agallocha	Eaglewood, agalwood	Juniperus macropoda	Himalayan juniper
Artemisia tibet.	Himalayan sage	Juniperus scopulorum	Juniper tips
Artemisia tridentata	Gray sage, desert sage, grey sage	Juniperus virginiana	Cedar wood, red cedar
Artemisia vulgaris	Mugwort,	Kaempferia galanga	Ginger lily
Boswellia carteri	Frankincense, olibanum	Laurus nobilis	Bay leaves
		Lavandula angustifolia	Lavender
Bursera graveolens	Palo santo	Ledum padesirere	Marsh tea, wild rosemary
Canarium luzonicum	Elemi		
Canarium strictum	Dammar	Myristica fragrans	Nutmeg
Cinnamomum camphora	Camphor	Myroxylon balsamum	Tolu balsam
Cinnamomum cecidodaphne	Sugandha kokila, fragrant cuckoo	Myrtus communis	Myrtle leaves
		Nardostachys jatamansi	Nard, spike nard
		Ocimum sanctum L.	Tulsi, Indian basil
Cinnamomum cassia	Cinnamon bark, cassia flowers	Peganum harmala	Syrian rue, harmel, wild rue
Cinnamomum tamala	Tejpat, teipat	Peumus boldus Mol.	Boldo
Cistus ladaniferus	Labdanum, labanum	Picea abies	Spruce resin, Burgundy resin
Commiphora abyssinica	Myrrh		
Commiphora erythraea	Opoponax, pastinaca opoponax	Pink damascena	Rose flowers
		Pinus sylvestris	Pine resin, colophonium
Commiphora mukul	Guggul, Indian Bdellium	Pistacia lenticus	Mastic
		Pogostemon patchouli	Patchouli
Coriandrum sativum	Coriander	Protium copal	Copal
Cymbopogon citratus	Lemon grass	Pterocarpus santalinus	Red sandalwood
Cyperus scariosus	Nut grass rhizome	Rosemarinus officinalis	Rosemary
Daemenorops draco	Dragon blood	Salvia apiana	White sage
Dipteryx odorata	Tonka bean	Salvia officinalis	Sage
Elettaria cardamomum	Cardamom	Santalum album	White sandalwood
Eriodictyon californicum	Yerba santa, bear plant	Saussurea lappa	Costus root
		Styrax benzoin	Loban, luban
Eucalyptus dives	Eucalyptus	Styrax calamitus	Styrax, storax
Eugenia caryophyllata	Clove	Styrax tonkinensis	Siam benzoin
Evernia prunastri	Oakmoss	Succinum	Amber
Ferula asafoetida	Asafoetida, asafetida	Tetraclinis articulata	Sandarac, Berber thuja
Ferula galbaniflua	Galbanum	Thuja occidentalis	Arbor vitae, thuja
Foeniculum vulgare	Fennel seeds	Thuja plicata	Cedar tips
Fumaria officinalis	Fumaria	Turnera diffusa Willd.	Damiana
Guaiacum officinale	Guaiacum wood	Verbena officinalis	Vervain
Hemidesmus indicus	Indian sarsaparilla	Vetiveria zizanoides	Vetiver, khus-khus
Hibiscus abelmusk	Sunset hibiscus seeds	Zantoxylum alatum	Zanthoxylum
Hierochloe odorata	Sweet grass	Zingiber officinale	Ginger

Index of Fragrance Messages

Every plant has a fragrance message of its own. This message contains a fundamental statement about how it can be used in our daily lives. It is an affirmation that is connected with the fragrance. When we establish contact with a fragrance we can easily activate this affirmation, feel it and carry it into our daily life.

The plants and their messages in this index are organized according to the elemental forces that are supportive in the particular application. The emphasis indicates the center of perception to which this fragrance has special access.

Fire/Emphasis	Fragrance Message
Amber/Mind	Renewal at the place of origin
Camphor/Body	Stepping forward and being strong
Cardamom/Emotion	Confidence and joy in life
Cassia Flowers/Emotion	Stepping out of constriction
Cinnamon Bark/Body	Food for the inner fire
Clove/Body	Approaching something new with momentum
Damiana/Emotion	Following the call of sensuality
Dragon Blood/Body	Strength and courage
Elemi/Mind	Setting out for new horizons
Eucalyptus/Body	Stepping out of swathes of fog into clarity
Frankincense/Body	Letting the truth in
Fumaria/Body	Reality or illusion
Galangal/Body	Aiming at the goal and being open to it
Ginger/Body	Life is movement
Ginger Lily/Emotion	Take advantage of the moment of lightness
Himalayan Juniper/Mind	Inner connection with the whole
Juniper Berries/Mind	Inner peace and trust
Juniper Tips/Mind	A presence that offers confidence
Lemon Grass/Mind	Welcome the new
Marsh Tea/Body	Powerful presence and ability to take action
Myrtle Leaves/Mind	Transparency and free vision
Nutmeg /Body	Everything is possible
Opoponax/Emotion	Completely in the here and now
Palo Santo/Emotion	Allowing the heart to become lighter
Red Sandalwood/Emotion	Serving in love
Rosemary/Mind	Taking action
Sandarac/Body	Clarity of the pure heart
Sugandha Kokila/Body	Will to action and assertiveness
Tejpat/Body	Setting off on new deeds
Zanthoxylum/Mind	Cheerfulness and assertiveness

Earth/Emphasis

	Fragrance Message
Angelica Root/Emotion	Walking your own path
Arbor Vitae/Body	Concentration on reality
Asafoetida/Mind	At the center of the cyclone
Cedar Tips/Emotion	Harmony grows out of a strong connection
Cedar Wood/Emotion	Protection and power are here
Costus Root/Emotion	Light in the dark
Eaglewood/Body	Completion and coming home
Galbanum/Emotion	Calmness and grounding develop
Gray Sage/Body	Preservation of life
Guaiacum Wood/Emotion	Sensitivity and strength are united here
Indian Sarsaparilla/Emotion	In good hands and supported
Myrrh/Emotion	Fertility and purity
Nard/Emotion	Finding the center
Nut-Grass Rhizome/Body	Strength from the center
Oakmoss/Body	Everything is one
Patchouli/Body	Basic trust and a strong presence
Vetiver/Body	Accepting and loving yourself
White Sandalwood/Emotion	The supportive foundation

Water/Emphasis

	Fragrance Message
Calamus Root/Emotion	Allowing sensitive perception
Coriander/Emotion	Creating equilibrium and calm
Fennel Seed/Emotion	Comfort and relaxation
Guggul/Emotion	Balsam for the wounded soul
Inula/Mind	Light from the root
Labdanum/Emotion	Discover the wonder of the senses
Lavender/Mind	Shedding light on the emotions
Loban/Emotion	Allow yourself to let go and surrender
Lupulin/Mind	Crossing the borders
Rose Flowers/Emotion	Understanding and forgiving
Siam Benzoin/Emotion	Balm for the wounded soul
Star Anise/Emotion	Let yourself fall and trust
Styrax/Emotion	Use this special moment
Sunset Hibiscus Seeds /Emotion	Feeling who you are
Sweet Grass/Emotion	Entering into harmony
Tolu Balsam/Emotion	Comfort and healing
Tonka Bean/Emotion	Enjoy and relax
White Sage/Body	Looking at what is essential

Air/Emphasis

	Fragrance Message
Bay Leaves/Mind	The eyes look ahead positively
Boldo/Mind	Healing absence of thoughts
Copal/Mind	Opening to the light
Dammar/Mind	Brightness flows through you
Gum Arabic/Emotion	Development of form through transparency
Himalayan Sage/Mind	Health, strength and long life
Mastic/Mind	Feeling contact with yourself
Mugwort/Body	Concentrating on the authentic
Pine Resin/Mind	Staying in the game
Sage/Body	Health, strength and longevity
Spruce Resin/Body	Passing on the light
Syrian Rue/Emotion	The seeker is guided to the light
Tulsi/Mind	Loving receptiveness
Vervain/Mind	Healing visions from the beyond
Yerba Santa/Body	Feeling love for yourself

List of Key Words
for theAromatic Plants

The traditions show diverse areas of application where experience has shown plants to be effective. These are summarized in the following list. They should be viewed as suggestions and a means of orientation when using the substances. They are not intended to be medical statements but should be understood as indications that impart a holistic picture of a plant's nature. From this perspective it is important to note that no form of application other than burning these substances as incense is recommended here.

Simply find the key word that describes your intent and select the substance which appears most interesting to you in the descriptions. Ultimately only your personal experience is what matters when you burn what you have selected as incense.

Anti-Depressive: Camphor, Cardamom, Eaglewood, Ginger Lily, Inula, Lemon Grass, Mastic, Nut Grass Rhizome, Opoponax

Anti-Fungal: Eaglewood, Sugandha Kokila

Aphrodisiac: Calamus Root, Cinnamon Bark, Clove, Coriander, Costus Root, Damiana, Guaiacum Wood, Guggul, Labdanum, Nut Grass Rhizome, Nutmeg, Patchouli, Rose, Sandalwood-Red, Sandalwood-White, Siam Benzoin, Sunset Hibiscus Seeds

Appetite Stimulating: Indian Sarsaparilla, Star Anise, Tonka Bean

Binders/Fixing Agents: Gum Arabic, Sandalwood-Red, Sandalwood-White

Birth Support: Syrian Rue

Calming/Soothing: Asafoetida, Eaglewood, Fennel, Guggul, Inula, Lavender, Sandarac, Star Anise, Styrax, Sunset Hibiscus Seed, Syrian Rue, Vetiver

Celebration: Cinnamon BarkInula, Star Anise, Sweet Grass, Tolu Balsam, Tonka Bean,

Changing the Mental State: Coriander, Dammar, Sage, Vervain, Zanthoxylum

Clairvoyance/Vision: Bay, Mastic, Copal, Dammar, Himalayan Juniper, Juniper Berries, Styrax, Syrian Rue, Vervain

Clearing of Thought/Emotions: Calamus Root, Cedar Tips, Eaglewood, Galbanum, Inula, Juniper Tips, Myrrh, Sage-White, Sandarac, Syrian Rue, Tulsi

Cold: Sandarac

Concentration: Arbor Vitae, Camphor, Mastic

Detoxification: Tulsi, Vetiver

Diabetes: Tejpat

Digestion: Angelica, Asafoetida, Bay Leaves, Boldo, Calamus Root, Cardamom, Cinnamon Bark, Costus Root, Fennel Seed, Galangal, Galbanum, Ginger, Guggul, Indian Sarsaparilla, Nut Grass Rhizome, Nutmeg, Rosemary, Sandarac, Star Anise, Styrax, Tejpat, Tulsi

Disinfection: Guggul, Himalayan Juniper, Myrrh, Myrtle, Opoponax, Pine Resin, Sandalwood-White

Ecstasy: Copal, Himalayan Juniper, Marsh Tea, Syrian Rue

Epilepsy: Amber, Galbanum, Vervain

Evening Incense: Eaglewood, Guggul, Sandalwood-White, Sandarac, Tolu Balsam

Euphoric: Cinnamon Bark, Damiana, Spruce Resin, Tonka Bean

Exorcism: Asafoetida, Fumaria, Himalayan Juniper

Eyesight: Fennel, Fumaria, Juniper Berries, Myrtle

Fertility: Angelica, Myrrh

Fever: Bay, Cardamom, Eucalyptus, Gray Sage, Indian Sarsaparilla, Lemon Grass, Nut-Grass Rhizome, Tejpat, Tonka Bean, Zanthoxylum

Grounding: Cedar Wood, Galbanum, Sandalwood-White, Vetiver,

Hallucinogen: Marsh Tea, Syrian Rue

Harmony: Cedar Wood, Cedar Tips, Loban, Myrtle, Opoponax, Palo Santo, Patchouli, Sweet Grass

Heart Opening: Amber, Cassia Flowers, Cinnamon Bark, Copal, Galangal, Labdanum, Mastic, Pine, Rose Flowers, Sandalwood-Red, Sweet Grass, Tonka Bean

Immune System, Strengthening: Bay, Eucalyptus, Juniper Tips, Lavender, Myrtle

Insect Repellant: Arbor Vitae, Camphor, Cassia Flowers, Cedar Wood, Clove, Costus Root, Gray Sage, Guggul, Himalayan Juniper, Lavender, Marsh Tea, Patchouli, Star Anise, Sugandha Kokila, Tonka Bean, Vetiver

Malaria: Tulsi

Meditation: Eaglewood, Frankincense, Sage-White, Sandalwood-White, Tolu Balsam, Vetiver

Menstruation: Cinnamon, Labdanum, Lupulin, Nard

Mental Disorders: Asafoetida, Boldo, Eaglewood

Mental Tonification: Angelica Root, Bay Leaves, Calamus Root, Copal, Dammar, Elemi, Nut Grass Rhizome, Rosemary, Sage

Morning Incense: Camphor, Elemi, Lemon Grass, Zanthoxylum

Narcotic: Costus Root, Marsh Tea, Star Anise, Tonka Bean

Nausea: Sandalwood-White

Nerve Strengthening: Boldo, Calamus Root, Camphor, Cardamom, Cinnamon Bark, Coriander, Costus Root, Eucalyptus, Frankincense, Galbanum, Ginger Lily, Guggul, Lemon Grass, Nard, Nut Grass Rhizome, Nutmeg, Vetiver, Zanthoxylum

Pain Relief: Boldo, Calamus Root, Clove, Copal, Coriander, Eucalyptus, Galbanum, Ginger, Gray Sage, Himalayan Sage, Lemon Grass, Myrrh, Myrtle, Rosemary, Sweet Grass, Tolu Balsam, Tulsi, Vervain, Zanthoxylum

Palliation: Coriander, Lavender, Sage-White, Star Anise, Styrax, Sweet Grass

Parasites: Juniper Berries

Polarization: Camphor, Fumaria, Marsh Tea, Sugandha Kokila

Protection: Amber, Angelica Root, Cedar Tips, Cedar Wood, Copal, Dammar, Himalayan Sage, Indian Sarsaparilla, Inula, Juniper Berries, Mugwort, Myrrh, Nutmeg, Opoponax, Spruce Resin, Tulsi, Vervain, Yerba Santa

Protection From Demons: Asafoetida, Copal, Dragon Blood, Fennel, Frankincense, Gray Sage, Himalayan Juniper, Inula, Juniper Berries, Mugwort, Palo Santo, Pine Resin, Rosemary, Sage, Tulsi, Vervain

Psychoactive: Bay, Gray Sage, Camphor, Cedar, Cinnamon Bark, Clove, Copal, Coriander, Damiana, Eaglewood, Juniper, Marsh Tea, Mugwort, Rosemary, Sage, Sage-White

Relaxation: Amber, Cassia Flowers, Cedar Wood, Cinnamon Bark, Coriander, Fennel, Loban, Lupulin, Mugwort, Palo Santo, Rose Flowers, Sandalwood-White, Sandarac, Styrax, Tolu Balsam, Tonka Bean

Respiratory Tract/Colds: Angelica, Calamus Root, Cedar Wood, Cinnamon Bark, Coriander, Costus Root, Damiana, Elemi, Frankincense, Galanga, Galbanum, Ginger Lily, Gray Sage, Guaiacum Wood, Himalayan Sage, Inula, Juniper Berries, Marsh Tea, Myrtle, Oakmoss, Pine Resin, Siam Benzoin, Rosemary, Sandarac, Sage, Sage-White, Star Anise, Styrax, Sweet Grass, Tejpat, Tolu Balsam, Tulsi, Sandalwood-White, Yerba Santa

Rheumatism: Angelica Root, Anise, Boldo, Cinnamon Bark, Frankincense, Galanga, Ginger, Guggul, Juniper Berries, Mugwort, Nutmeg, Spruce Resin, Star Marsh Tea, Tolu Balsam, Yerba Santa

Room Clearing: Boldo, Copal, Dammar, Elemi, Eucalyptus, Frankincense, Himalayan Juniper, Juniper Tips, Lavender, Palo Santo, Sage-White, Sandarac, Vervain,

Sexual Tonic: Asafoetida, Cinnamon Bark, Mugwort, Vervain,

Sleep Promoting: Amber, Boldo, Lavender, Lupulin, Marsh Tea, Nard

Stimulating/Activating: Bay, Camphor, Elemi, Eucalyptus, Galanga, Ginger, Ginger Lily, Pine, Lemon Grass, Suganda Kokila, Tejpat, Zanthoxylum

Support for the Dying: Eaglewood, Himalayan Sage, Mugwort, Oakmoss, Spruce Resin, Sandalwood-White

Tonification: Angelica Root, Arbor Vitae, Cedar Wood, Cedar Tips, Clove, Dragon Blood, Fennel, Gray Sage, Indian Sarsaparilla, Mastic, Mugwort, Pine Resin, Spruce Resin, Vetiver

Trance/Ritual: Marsh Tea, Syrian Rue, Sage-White

Transformation: Amber, Eaglewood, Himalayan Sage, Mugwort, Oakmoss,

Trust, Developing: Amber, Cedar Tips, Fennel, Galangal, Indian Sarsaparilla, Patchouli, Rose Flowers, Sandalwood-White, Star Anise, Sweet Grass, Vervain, Yerba Santa

Venereal Disease: Boldo, Guaiacum Wood

Will, Strengthening: Ginger, Gray Sage, Juniper Berries, Marsh Tea, Nutmeg, Rosemary, Sugandha Kokila

Witchcraft: Fumaria, Inula, Juniper Berries, Marsh Tea, Styrax, Vervain

About the Author

Thomas Kinkele was born in Germany in 1949. After he finished school, he spent three years traveling "on the road" throughout the world. In 1975, he established the *flora perpetua* company that initially worked only with the decorative processing of botanic materials. This led him to the fragrances of the plant kingdom in the Eighties.

His continuous search for the deeper connections took him on the inner journey from Sidharta to Yogananda to the *Tibetan Book of the Dead* and on to an intensive phase with Castaneda. He began practicing the Rosecrucianism at the beginning of the Eighties, which was then followed by sweat-hut and self-awareness work. Then he found Jabrane Mohamed Sebnat and the enneagram in 1990, a teacher who led him to his spiritual homeland through the Sufi Path of the Heart.

From 1996 to 1998 he trained in aromatology/osmology with Martin Henglein (ISAO). During all of these stages, he always has worked with incense. Thomas Kinkele currently holds lectures and gives seminars and experiential workshops with essential oils and incense.

You can contact Thomas Kinkele at: thomas@floraperpetua.de

• Natural Europe Enterprises, PO Box 7207, Chico, CA 95927, USA
www.NaturalEurope.com, service@NaturalEurope.com, contact person: Michael Wrightson

carries and distributes incenses, aroma smoke products, and accessories from Thomas Kinkele's European company *flora perpetua*

• A broad line of aromatic substances and utensils are also available at:
www.internatural.com